# New Directions in Teaching English Language

A Discovery Approach

by William B Currie

Director, Colchester English Study Centre;
formerly Head of Applied Linguistics,
Jordanhill, Glasgow

Longman

Longman Group Limited, London

Associated companies, branches, and
representatives throughout the world

First published 1973

ISBN 0 582 55071 8

We are grateful to Mrs Iris Wise,
Macmillan London and Basingstoke,
The Macmillan Company of Canada
Limited and Macmillan Publishing Co., Inc.
of New York for reproduction of
'The Main Deep' from *Collected Poems*
by James Stephens. Reprinted with
permission of Macmillan Publishing Co., Inc.
from *Collected Poems* by James Stephens.
Copyright 1925, 1926 by The Macmillan Company,
renewed 1953, 1954 by James Stephens.

Printed in Great Britain by
Richard Clay (The Chaucer Press), Ltd,
Bungay, Suffolk

# Contents

# Preface

At a time when the discussion of the place of Language in Education and Learning thrives on the variety of contenders for the place vacated by Grammar, it is more than ever necessary to relate this debate to its historical setting, to identify for the teacher the areas of specialist knowledge from which his own position must derive, and to put forward practical proposals for new approaches to the study of Language in schools which rest on investigation, experience and research.

In this opening contribution to the *Applied Linguistics and Language Study* series, Dr. Currie makes plain that the changes he intends to the mother tongue curriculum stem from the need 'to develop a deeper cultural awareness in pupils of the use of Language in society'. Such changes must arise from the combination of historical documentation, analysis of relevant linguistic and educational-psychological research, and, what for the teacher is central, tested procedures in selected classrooms.

If we point out that it is only through the teacher and the learner of Language that the application of such research can be decided, and if we are also suspicious that classroom learning realities are such that any doctrinaire and simplistic transfer of the results of formal research will more burden than assist, then we throw squarely on the teacher a difficult eclecticism. Sensible changes to curricula demand from the teacher-initiator governed awareness of applicable research.

From his central position of the need for change in the teaching of Language the author develops the treatment of a number of important topics : the relationship between knowledge of Language in the psychological sense and its performance in the social sense ; the differing roles of teacher, linguist/psychologist and learner in respect of Language study ; the conflict between 'academic' syllabuses and the need to develop the learner's ability to function linguistically in society beyond the school.

As readers will be aware, these important topics for the teacher of Language have often been lost in the competitive welter between linguistic and psychological theories. While sensibly referring to the respectable history of such academic debate, Dr. Currie steers the reader clearly through the thickets of theory, and in underlining the view that many teachers will share, that language acquisition is a continuing process throughout the school, shows that it is premissed on the need to develop the learner's personal and creative responses to language in use.

These responses to the cognitive and social aspects of Language and language discovery are made explicit in the final section of the book where the author's views on 'rhetoric in a new key' are illustrated and substantiated with references to experimental materials and evaluative tests.

Christopher N Candlin
General Editor
Applied Linguistics and Language Study.

# Introduction and Acknowledgement

This is a book for teachers of English and its central theme is the relationship between what we know about language and what we know about the native speaker. On the one hand we have a body of knowledge about language, linguistics, and on the other we have what we might describe as shafts of insight in psychology, sociology and education illuminating aspects of the native speaker as a language learner. As teachers, however, our knowledge of the native speaker does not necessarily resolve itself into statements of one or other of the sciences; it is a knowledge of pupils, their lives and their practical problems of school learning.

If a simple linear relationship existed between linguistics as a body of knowledge and what a pupil learns about language in class, there would be little need to present teachers with more than the best available grammar and ask them to teach it by fair means or foul. In the past, in fact, there were cases where little more than this was done in the name of language teaching in our secondary schools. Since about the end of the second world war, however, there has been a growing awareness that straightforward learning of grammar and factual testing of that knowledge is an empty operation. A wider, deeper and more humane view has developed of the place and context of mother-tongue education in a school setting. It is in this context that this study is undertaken together with discussion of developments in the science of language itself.

The body of knowledge which we refer to loosely as linguistics is in fact a complex of disciplines. For example, it embraces general linguistics, which deals with theories of language, applied linguistics which links linguistic theory with numerous fields of investigation such as language learning; more accurately defined fields of applied linguistic study include psycholinguistics, linking questions of psychology with linguistics, and sociolinguistics, linking questions of sociology with those of linguistics. In the last three decades, the whole world of linguistics has been rapidly developing. An unprecedented upsurge of interest in linguistics within universities,

8

spilling over into education and other fields, has resulted. A vast collection of books and articles on language and language learning has emerged, and it is not surprising to find that teachers have often found that even their most sincere efforts to study linguistic publications in the hope of reorientating themselves to the problems of the syllabus have been daunted.

It is precisely to help with that situation that this book is offered. The point of origin of the whole study is the classroom, and the focus is on our aims and methods in the language syllabus for native speakers of English. Our two main principles in this study are that reform of the syllabus should stem from the known needs of the schools and that innovation in the syllabus should be backed up by appropriate research. The book is, of course, only one teacher's view of the developments referred to, but this has the advantages that particular practical experience of teaching English language has led to directed enquiries in linguistics, and to a school experiment involving the writing of a new type of course and experimental evaluation of the work.

The work which is reflected in this book extended over some five years of study and research and I must acknowledge the extensive help and encouragement of many colleagues over that period. The main study was conducted when I was on the staff of Jordanhill College of Education, Glasgow. The Principal and Governors of the college arranged for me to spend a period of full time study in the Department of Applied Linguistics, Edinburgh, and afterwards, as head of Applied Linguistics at Jordanhill, I was given facilities to carry out further research and to conduct the school experiment referred to. I am particularly indebted to Sir Henry Wood, Principal of Jordanhill, for his interest and help. I would also like to record my indebtedness to Professor S. P. Corder, and Dr. Alan Davies for their stimulus and encouragement during my doctoral studies in Edinburgh University; to Dr. George Davie for his counsel on rhetoric; to Dr. A. E. Pilliner for his invaluable advice on the statistical side of the experiment and to Professor M. A. K. Halliday for his direct and indirect stimulus, and to his research team in University College, London.

I would particularly like to thank the teachers in the seven experimental schools for their part in the experiment, and to express my gratitude to the Heads of Department, Headmasters and Directors of Education concerned who gave the experiment their blessing. I should like also to record the stimulus I found in the discussions and conferences of the S.E.D. Central Committee on English, under its chairman, Dr. W. A. Gatherer, H.M.I. In the compilation of the book itself I should like to thank Mrs. Geraldine Bachmann and Mrs. E. Mitsidou, both of Athens, for their practical help with the script. Lastly, I would like to record my surprise and pleasure that my wife and family have managed to endure with such good will living with the mounds of manuscript, tests and course materials the work of the last five years has produced.

# 1 The Aim of a Mother-tongue Language Course

The definition of an aim for the teaching of English language to native speaker pupils can prove to be a difficult operation. The pupil already possesses a socially acceptable operational control of English; if he lacked this he would not be at a normal school. English is the medium of his instruction throughout the school; English is the vehicle of his culture, the basis of much of his manners, a foundation of his humour; it may contribute to his sense of nationalism and to his idea of social class. In view of the importance of these issues in the life of the pupil, it is not surprising to find that teachers of English have often felt that their educational duty lay in establishing the skills of English which could play a key part in enriching the social and cultural lives of their pupils. It is our view that in approaching this high goal mother-tongue language teaching has over-stressed the training of native speakers at the expense of developing a deeper, cultural awareness in pupils of the use of language in society.

One underlying cause of this problem of goal is a strong belief among English teachers, in schools and universities, that specific transfer of training takes place between a knowledge of grammar rules – or the rules of rhetoric, phonology, spelling, etc. – and an ability to perform effectively in the skills of language. If one is to believe the introductions of English course books over the last hundred years, grammar has seriously been suggested as the knowledge necessary for the correction of speech and writing, for the improvement of composition, for the development of character and for the understanding of literary and non-literary works in the language. The case put has been a simple one, that one can teach A (grammar rules, etc.) and test B (composition, speech, comprehension, etc.). If the transfer is positive, the more one teaches A the better will be the performance in B.

In one or other of its forms this belief lies behind memoranda on the teaching of English until very recent years; it also lies behind typical complaints made in the annual reports on education where an inspector might report that classes seemed to know their grammar, but were poor writers of English, expressing pained surprise that this should be the case. At a school syllabus level, remedial work in English skills has often been thought of in the past as more or clearer study of the rules of grammar or of rhetoric.

It is not our argument here that it is entirely ineffective to teach skills in this way. Without doubt, there are bodies of rules which to a degree are reflected in the skills of English; further, there are certain pupils who learn readily via rules. It would be foolish to argue that there are no links between our knowledge about language and our performance in language. It is our view, however, that these links are unlikely to be simple linear transfer between rules and performance. Further, such classroom research as we have on this topic not only suggests that simple assumptions of transfer are inconclusive within their own experimental brief, but that several studies in this field have shown inhibition of creative skills of language resulting from training in rules.

Some of the available evidence might be of interest. Early papers by Hoyt (1906) and Rapeer (1913) bring cumulative evidence to show that the simple notion of transfer between pupils' knowledge of grammar and their abilities to produce written English is not supported by evidence. Segel and Barr (1926) came to the firm conclusion that 'formal grammar has no transfer value as far as applied grammar is concerned'. Symonds (1931) re-subjected several of these earlier papers to experimental tests, using a technique of studying the pupils' ability to correct errors. He *did* find a small indication of transfer between grammar drilling and error correction, but it was so small a gain, he argued, for such hard drilling, that it seemed worthless as a school method. Symonds reported that he thought the quality of grammar drills used and the intelligence of the pupils had been responsible for the gains.

Many teachers in Scotland are familiar with the work of Macauley (1947) *The Difficulty of Grammar*. This is a very practical study carried out in Glasgow to investigate the complaints of teachers that pupils from primary schools where grammar had been taught extensively had 'complete lack of understanding of even the terms of grammar after four years' teaching'. Macauley tested in the primary school, the junior secondary and the senior secondary schools, following a group of pupils through. He tested for the recognition of five parts of speech as labels for underlined words in use in sentences, with

12

one word only tested in each sentence. He showed that the ability of pupils to recognise the word class of an item used in text was low at the end of four years' primary school training, dropped in the first year of the secondary school, including the case of the best streams, and only by the end of the third year senior secondary school (grammar school selected) – a double language course – were scores approaching competence recorded: 41.5% of pupils were able to score 50% or more right answers in all five parts of speech tested. In his summary he spoke of grammar in the primary school and in all but the senior academic streams of the secondary school being 'so much hocus pocus' to the pupils. His conclusion was that relating grammar to the language in use by word classification was too difficult for the pupils, therefore no transfer could be expected.

Other studies include Robinson (1960) who showed that there was no evidence of correlation between ability to perform in grammar and composition ability, and Harris (1962, 1965) who showed that the study of English grammar had a negligible or even a relatively harmful effect on the correctness of children's writing in the early secondary school. On correlation between knowledge and productive skill he held 'There is no greater correlation between grammatical knowledge and English skills than between two totally unrelated subjects. Indeed, correlations between say arithmetic and grammar are often higher than between grammar and composition.'

Teachers who maintain that knowledge of grammar will produce results in skills are either maintaining the view against this and other negative evidence, or are criticising either the theory behind these investigations or the methods of the individual experiments. There are strong grounds for rejecting the simple associative chain theory that lies behind the assumptions of this learning transfer. While it is beyond the scope of this book to investigate this aspect of psychology in detail we offer the following points for consideration. Learning a language skill may not in fact be different from other learning at all; it may be making use of generic coding devices similar to those used in any understanding and memorisation we undertake (see Chapter 6). One finds more and more acceptance for the notion of the 'seamless robe of learning'. More specifically one finds psycho-linguistics unwilling to make experimental distinctions between linguistic competence and general intellectual competence. A similar complaint is made that there is a confusion between linguistic competence (as internalised knowledge lying behind the production of speech) and mechanism (the intellectual means producing language behaviour) (see Lyons and Wales (eds.) 1966:156–163). In brief, while some pupils to our certain knowledge seem to be able to learn how to do B by learning about A, they are not paradigms for a review of school learning of the mother-tongue.

In our view, the aims of teaching English as a mother-tongue in schools are no different in their essence from the general intellectual aims of education. Gleason's dictum is well worth our study: 'An educated man should be able to think rationally and incisively about his environment and about his human situation' (1964:267). This general principle might be said to be as valid for the sciences as for the arts. Biology is rational and incisive about the natural environment and we turn to it for explanations and experimental proof in its sphere; mathematics is rational and incisive about the nature of our environment in terms of quantities and numerical and symbolic values and relationships. In the academic disciplines, linguistics is, likewise, the rationalisation of our knowledge about the human language environment. We take up the view here, that *an educated native speaker ought to be able to be rational and articulate about the nature of his mother-tongue and about the relationships which exist between the user of the language and his society.*

This is a wide, general aim which might embrace syllabus commitments ranging from considerable detail of pronunciation, writing and grammar to questions of style and literary quality, wherever articulate discussion of specific language features is deemed to be appropriate. We would stress 'wherever appropriate'. Between the framing of the general aim and the effective implementation of the principle in practice falls the responsibility of judgement. This responsibility of judgement may be seen to rest with syllabus reformers, with teacher trainers, subject committees and other bodies, but in the final and vital analysis the teacher is the judge of what aspects of language in use a pupil ought to be concerned with describing. He is the one who will, in Firth's words, 'make our young people actively and critically aware of the sort of language which is used for them and against them every day of their lives' (1964:108).

There is another very important aspect of the teaching aim, however. A teacher should not think of himself as feeding-in knowledge when he uses appropriate pieces of linguistic description. Rather, he should think of himself as rationalising what mother-tongue speaking pupils are already aware of in

14

performance terms. Pupils come into class rich in language. They have already learned it well; if they had not they would not be accepted as normal children in a normal socio-linguistic community, and they would not be in our classes. This does not mean that they all know how to spell, punctuate, write sentences or give the meanings of English in use. But it does mean that they have an internalised knowledge of the language itself, its sound system, its intonation and stress, its underlying and surface meanings and its latent and overt organisation in grammar. Thus, a teacher, in making articulate, intelligible and communicable an aspect of description, must try to draw out of the pupil his own underlying awareness of that aspect of language in use. Further, he must never offer a description of an aspect of language which teacher and pupil alike feel to be untrue to the nature of the tongue.

An aim is the first necessary step towards the revision of a syllabus. While it is made independent of questions of linguistic theory, learning theory or method, there can be no doubt that these and other forces operating on the syllabus are very important for our case. Further, the school syllabus is a product of history and we are conscious that each step that has been taken in its formation has reflected the knowledge and philosophy of the time. In the chapters which follow, we give consideration to past and present forces on language education which, in our view, must be taken into account in syllabus reform. Finally, we hope by bringing together an account of this sort, with detailed proposals for a language course, we may help teachers to focus more clearly on the complicated issues which face mother-tongue education today.

# 2 The School Grammar Debate

The teaching of English grammar in British schools is a tradition of long standing, related to the still older tradition of the study of Latin and Greek grammar, which our label 'Grammar School' refers to. This span of grammar study deserves our interest, even our awe, since it has persisted and has coloured our educational systems for almost as long as organised education has existed here. From the point of view of syllabus reform in English, however, we take the modest view that mother-tongue study of grammar in our schools has something like a hundred years of practice behind it. For example, in Scotland, although there is local evidence of grammar being prominent in the study of English before the dates I refer to below, we should think of grammar taking a real hold of mother-tongue study about the mid-nineteenth century. Two dates in particular are important, 1864, when English was raised to a status in the syllabus equal to that of Latin or Greek (at least for examination purposes) and 1888 when the first national public examination in English was instituted. By 1888 English had largely won its fight for official recognition as a school subject leading to examinations at the highest school level, but this status was modified by two influences, closely related to each other. One, a practical contingency, was that the classics master still taught English; secondly, the enormous prestige of traditional rhetoric was brought to bear on English studies and a strongly classical direction of language study was advocated. Something of the detailed position taken up by rhetoric is discussed in Chapter 7. We should remember as an added factor that in the mid-nineteenth century teachers of English were often appointed to the grammar schools by examination in Latin, not in the native tongue they would speak and teach in. These influences have, in some measure, conditioned the whole field of English study up to the present day.

Teachers might be thought of as being under the influence of three main pressures in their reforms of mother-tongue language study. Internally, they have been subjected to inspection in the schools, and from time to time in the annual reports of the inspectorate there have been extended references to the teaching of English as a subject. Sometimes these references have been given the status of official memoranda or reports designed to guide teachers in their work; other official reports on English teaching have been produced by working parties, special committees and so on – often giving us a good indication of the state of the subject in terms of curricular development.

Externally, the syllabus in English has been under the influence of university thinking on language study. Not only are graduate teachers likely to promote the academic viewpoint of their own studies at university, but many of the best teachers retain a strong interest in their subject fields and are members of learned societies through which university directions in language study reach the classroom. Finally, lay opinion has often strong ideas about the relationship between school language study and social questions, and through education committees, churches and, not least, parents, certain socio-linguistic values are often pressed on to the teacher. Teachers may therefore be thought of as, on the one hand, extensions of the universities, and on the other, as social and moral educators expected to produce for society the kind of language user thought to be desirable.

The memoranda and reports of the inspectorate in Britain form a very interesting field of study. They represent the official view of Her Majesty's Inspectors at a given time, but the documents are not law in the sense that they are legally binding either on the writers or the teachers. There is no equivalent in Britain of the official syllabuses one finds in European countries, and elsewhere, where teachers are not free to reject official guidance if they disapprove of it. The flexibility and freedom that this brings to British education has the great advantage that internal reform goes as quickly as the teachers themselves want it to go, but it has the disadvantage that obvious entrenchment and reactionary teaching cannot easily be stopped officially. In our view, the tensions between classroom reforms, prompted since about 1950 by a rapidly changing university scene, and attitudes of entrenchment persisting from the existing grammatical traditions of the schools have led in the last decade or so to an uneasy agnosticism in the teaching of English language. On the one side, university and college language study seems to be burgeoning; on the other, no extensive school syllabus reforms in language study have yet provided the teacher with a body of classroom practice to replace traditional courses. While many of us are highly optimistic on this last point, feeling that

17

the publications of the Schools Council in England, and the Central Committee on English in Scotland mark the source of a British school reform of some moment, at the time of writing in both England and Scotland a high degree of uncertainty still typifies the thinking of many teachers of English language.

Many teachers, clinging to older classroom traditions and scholarship, (and perhaps also to existing official memoranda) find many of the new directions suggested by linguistics bewildering. For instance, some teachers, albeit with a sense of guilt, insist on teaching traditional formal grammar as part of the course of language study; others have decided to abandon grammar teaching altogether, while remaining uneasily aware that no substitute for this rationalisation of language structure is available, or if available, is not generally acceptable to schools. Few passages from official documents illustrate the basis of the teacher's dilemma more clearly than Struthers' 1907 primary school memorandum:

'Grammar owes its place in the elementary curriculum not to its method, which is not peculiar to it, but to its subject matter, which is of universal interest. It is taught because the discipline which it affords is needful or at least helpful to the right use and understanding of language. Only so much grammar need be taught as can thus be applied: the phenomena treated should be such as can arise naturally in reading and writing; but the systematic instruction in its principles, so far as is required, should be given in regular grammar lessons.' (1907:207)

In this key passage, with its strangely modern ring, we detect the attractiveness for the teacher in his role of scholar, of the philosophy of grammar, which might link the study and teaching of language with the sciences and with philosophy and mathematics. Struthers is careful to point out, however, that practical issues relating to the reading and writing of language and of comprehension should be given priority in selecting the content and teaching techniques of the language syllabus. It would seem that scholarly studies of grammar may be in conflict with the general aims of education, the literacy and the social development of the pupil. One can almost detect the sigh with which the 'universal interest' of the subject matter of grammar is rejected in favour of a pragmatically justified concern with school performance in English. Throughout Europe one finds this issue still the vital one; many academically inclined teachers worry about the intellectual value of schoolwork. In general the pre-occupation with the more abstract 'intellectual' qualities of instruction dominates the syllabus in countries which have not adopted 'child-centred' school programmes. Thus Greece, France, certain parts of Germany and Poland teach a high proportion of formal analysis as the mainstay of their mother-tongue programmes and feel that they are cheating, intellectually, if they do not. In Britain there is a subtler, but equally deep-rooted reliance on formal grammar in English work in present-day Scotland, and in Wales, and the publication of such books as *Why Tommy isn't Learning* by Stuart Froome suggests that all is not well with the English programmes of liberal England. Froome argues that decline in school performance is directly relatable to our drift away from intellectual training through rules, including the rules of formal grammar (1970:40, etc.).

There is a further aspect of the modern teaching dilemma in Struthers' passage. If practical aims dominate in the English language syllabus, and if they are somehow related to a study of grammar, how much grammar and of what sort ought a teacher to teach? Ignoring for the moment the assumption that grammar teaching *does* produce the practical ends required, we see that teachers are required (as is usual in Britain) to decide for them-selves the nature and extent of their grammar teaching. The free-dom of this choice could be the basis of valuable teacher-based reform, and it is in Scotland, but it has the enormous drawback that, if the body of teachers is unable to think its way towards a syllabus, textbooks of a comprehensive and authoritarian sort are likely to direct the teaching of language. It is almost as though the intellectual status of the teacher and the quality of teacher training were being wagered against doctrinaire and slavish textbook following in the classroom. One suspects that in 1907 the reference to systematic instruction in the principles of gram-mar and the use of regular grammar lessons obscured and out-weighed the parenthetical phrase 'so far as is required'.

The history of this is interesting for us today. An obvious struggle over the nature and place of school grammar was waged in the first two decades of the twentieth century in both England and Scotland. The nineteenth century had seen orthography, etymology and syntax embraced as school grammar study, and under the influence of classics and rhetoric these aspects of English language study were tackled in most secondary schools (age 12 plus) and by perhaps the four top years of the primary school. Orthography became the well-known spelling lesson, and either from the spelling list, or from the reading book, a dictionary-and-derivation study of words emerged. Grammar became a separate lesson from reading, involved with the facts of syntax and word parsing. These language lessons were taught, not as Struthers had suggested, incidentally, but as expository lessons teaching the rational nature of traditional grammar — or at least traditional school grammar, as proposed by course-book writers like Nesfield (1898, 1912, etc.) Rote exercises and tests on the facts of grammar were common, and most teachers were convinced of the positive value for the performance of reading and writing skills of the abstract study of grammatical principles.

The state of school grammar teaching in England and Scotland raised, among teaching organisations, a far-reaching concern with the nature of school grammar. Prompted by the growing strength of this concern the Classical Association of Great Britain became sponsors of the Joint Committee on Grammatical Terminology (1908–11) chaired by Professor Sonnenschein, whose brief was 'to consider the terminology used in the teaching of languages, ancient and modern, including English, commonly studied in English schools, in the hope of framing some simplified and consistent scheme of grammatical nomenclature, tending in the direction of uniformity for all the languages concerned'.

The Joint Committee included classicists, professional linguists, teachers of foreign languages, academics of English studies and certain foreign observers. They received over a hundred detailed accounts of the confusions in teaching arising from grammatical terminology, and by 1909 they were able to circulate an interim report. Comments on this from informed sources, led to a final report in 1911. There were reservations to this report expressed by certain members of the committee, some unspecified, but most detailed. For example Professor Conway, a classicist, objected to the terms Noun Clause, Adjective Clause, and Adverb Clause and he insisted that pronouns and nouns in English must be shown to have case, even if only pronouns are inflected in the majority of examples. Seven out of twenty-four signatories of the report noted reservations, and six members of the committee produced an addendum which amounted to a major reservation (in the form of a regret) over the handling of French pronouns. But, all in all, the results would seem to be as nearly unanimous as we could expect from a group of scholars and teachers with such widely different backgrounds and interests.

For about a decade afterwards (interrupted by the Great War) there was considerable debate in both England and Scotland of the Report of 1911. The issues resolved themselves as one of principle – whether the committee has forced the description of modern languages, including English, into too classical a mould. The chairman of the committee, Professor Sonnenschein, a classicist, felt moved to collect evidence for a display of public support for the committee's findings and, in 1922, he wrote to all the associations represented on the 1911 committee asking for their support for the findings of the 1911 Report a decade after their publication. The English Association was among those asked, and they formally gave their support. Sonnenschein then wrote to the press on receiving formal support from the original participants, and then announced that there was *unanimous* approval for his findings. The consternation that this caused in the ranks of the English Association resulted in many meetings, conferences and pamphlets which brought to light a profound feeling among practising teachers that Latinate terminology for English grammar was a grave mistake, and further that the teaching of grammar as such in schools was out of touch with the aims of English education.

A sub-committee of the English Association was set up in 1922 and it published a note expressly disapproving of the pro-classical tone of Sonnenschein's Report, and in a key sentence they set the target for what was to be the subsequent pre-occupation of at least three decades of English teachers, both in England and Scotland. '(The English Association) desires, therefore, to explain that its assent to the recommendations of the report has been given with reservations, and to express its belief that teachers who keep abreast of modern linguistic and grammatical research will be careful not to prejudice investigations by using in their English lessons any term borrowed from the conditions of other languages unless it can be justified by the occurrence of similar conditions in our own' (1923:6).

This important remark may be seen as a protest against a prescriptive and idealistic approach to grammar work in schools. It is in tune with the scientific approaches of the early years of the twentieth century; an objective, descriptive and, one might argue, positivistic point of view is embraced by the statement. But from the practical point of view it seemed to the Association and to practising teachers that it was unsatisfactory that old gods should be thrown down and new gods set up in their place without proper school investigation – a point most modern teachers of English would applaud. The Association sponsored a conference at Bedford College, London, in 1922, a conference representing both academic and teaching opinion on language teaching in schools and published as a pamphlet, *The Problem of Grammar* (1923), two important papers from the conference. This was designed to stimulate teachers in the constructive task of proposing a 'pure or functional grammar of English' for guidance of teachers and use in schools.

In *The Problem of Grammar*, Professor A. Mawer, a linguist, stressed the 'vast and essential' differences between English and Latin grammar. The 'weakening' of English from a moderately inflected language to a minimally inflected language was, he argued, neither simplification nor corruption. But changes in a language of this order called for changes in descriptive technique. His dictum was that as morphology and accidence become less prominent, syntax becomes proportionately more prominent and he held that the linguistic study that bodies such as Sonnenschein's committee had produced had failed to reflect this change. Further, he maintained that a language like Latin, which was not spoken as a living language and was therefore unchanging would be better described by its rules, while English, a living changing language, required an ordered account of what we might hear spoken every day. Clearly, Mawer took up a corpus-centred, descriptive standpoint very much in the tradition described by Sweet as the British tradition of linguistics, 'Our tendency is not so much towards the antiquarian philology and text-criticism in which German scholars have done so much, as towards *the observation of the phenomena of living languages* . . .' (1877).

Andrews, who contributed the second paper in the Association's pamphlet (1923) put forward a pragmatic, classroom viewpoint, very much orientated to the needs of the child. He asked teachers to decide first of all why they ought to teach grammar, and, if they felt they had to, to decide what that grammar ought to be. It is interesting to find Andrews seriously questioning the notion of transfer of training from grammar to correct speech ; he implied that it was ludicrous to propose that the best way of learning something was to study something else. His view was that the grammar we should use in schools should be 'pure grammar', which he was quite prepared to call 'universal grammar'. In detail this turns out to be subject/predicate clause analysis, noun identification and noun phrase modification ; verb identification and verb phrase modification. Essentially

Andrews proposed not a formal grammar, as his term 'pure' might mislead us into thinking, but a grammar of function, on a notional basis. This places him close to the view we find at the present time in many schools attempting to review their language teaching programmes.

We should particularly note Andrews' goals for grammar teaching. He expected that pupils would gain from a study of grammar what they would gain from a study of any other science (*sic*) – *that the manifold of their experience could be reduced to order*, that is, that it could be classified and generalised. Thus grammar might be seen as a child's first lesson in science. Secondly, he expected that the pupil, once he had seen that the language was structured, would surmise from his own experience that structures have functions. Andrews was an experienced teacher and he knew that his proposals would succeed or fail not so much on their philosophy, but on the teaching methods by which they were used. He was careful, because of this, to advocate grammar as an enlightened and enlightening tool for the elucidation of interesting texts, and to denounce dull drills of grammar for grammar's sake.

We have included these details of Andrews' paper partly because of their historical importance, but also because of the insightful modern proposals they contain. His paper, in our view, contributed solidly to innovation and reform in English language work in England and was circulated by members of the English Association in Scotland both between the wars and in the post-second world war years.[1] Ironically, a pamphlet with so much to say for the better teaching of grammar may have contributed to the rejection of grammar which took place in England within five years of the Bedford College conference. But from our point of view Andrews is a basis from which we might argue for grammar to be *taught*. His points on technique as opposed to theory are directly in line with modern classroom reform; his insightful reference to grammar as a rationalising device with heuristic re-discovery value is taken up in detail later in this book (Chapter 7) and is supported; finally, his general view that English, like other subjects, is concerned with reducing the world of experience to intellectually appreciated order, is most attractive to those of us who believe that one of the duties of an education system is to produce people who are rationally and articulately aware of their environment, including the environment of language.

In England, in the twenties, grammar rapidly fell from grace.

23

A small resurgence of interest in grammar can be traced in the official reports of 1927, but this was sharply rejected immediately afterwards. In Scotland, grammar appears to have been subjected to some criticism in the years immediately after the end of the first world war, since in 1924, Dr. Stewart, H.M.I., made a long reference in the Annual Report on how grammar might be taught as a humanity. He specifically noted that the subject had been 'repatriated after a period of ostracism'. But his view is reactionary, both in its linguistics and in its advocacy of method.

In a very interesting lecture on *The Grammarian and his Material*, given in Scotland in 1930, J. M. Wattie, who had himself risen to be H.M. Senior Chief Inspector of Schools stated his considered view on grammar as a school subject. He had openly rejoiced in 1927 when there had been a small resurgence in England of the interest in grammar, and in Scotland a consolidation of tradition. 'Grammar is fully restored to favour,' he wrote in the Scottish Education Report for 1927, 'though shorn of a good deal of its former elaboration'. Wattie's main concern in his 1930 paper was for correctness, one of the aspects of English language study which has had an extraordinary hold in Scottish education since the 'new manner' of English speech began to replace Scots in the eighteenth century. A degree of liberalism appears in Wattie's remarks, for example a growing realisation of the importance of spoken forms in language study, but he is still very conservative about the status of grammar. Even if it can be shown, he argues, that the role of the grammarian is merely to record, to observe and not to sit in judgement on the language, this descriptive attitude can never be the attitude of the schools, 'for the simple reason that in every department of the school work (I say particularly in grammar) effective pedagogy necessarily calls for a certain degree of dogmatism'.

'A certain degree of dogmatism' is well shown in some syllabuses for English in the 1930s. For example, one was devised by the Scottish Council for Research in Education, contemporary with Wattie's remarks, for the 'Advanced Division' – age 12–15 junior secondary school, whose pupils, of course, were not intellectually able and were streamed below academic grades. It gives in detail a full subject-and-predicate sentence analysis for these pupils. But it is also superficially liberal. Parsing is pruned down from a requirement that *every* word should be parsed in full to the advice that only the main ones should be parsed for part of speech and principal relationships.

24

Further, for the slower pupils in the 'Advanced Division', it was thought unwise to stress too much work on verbs of incomplete predication. When we recall that this course was for pupils who had *not* been promoted to academic courses in the secondary school, we might well be forgiven for wondering what academic pupils would have been recommended to study in the grammar lesson. In all probability they would have been required to undergo a full grammar-rhetoric programme such as might have been specified for Scottish schools at any time from the days of Bain (1869, etc.) onwards. Further, the methods proposed by the 1931 document depend on exposition of grammatical principle and appropriate exercises, placing a considerable emphasis on abstract grammar in the work.

The climate of grammar work obtaining in the thirties in Scotland, while it may have been more doctrinaire than in England, almost certainly characterises the teaching situation generally. A debate was in progress proposing reform of the grammar syllabus, but it seems clear that there was a widespread adherence to traditional ideas especially in the public schools and grammar schools, and in its essence English teaching was not substantially different in the thirties from the methods of the preceding fifty years. There were, of course, progressive measures at work in the thirties in education, but the depressed state of the profession, with problems of unemployment of teachers, and stagnation of promotion led to a climate in which most teachers were prepared rather to perpetuate tradition as it was found in the prescribed books of a given department, than to experiment and introduce new directions of study. The second world war effectively prevented reform during the early forties, but it also produced in the immediate post-war years a freshness and a willingness to change which had not been possible before.

An early post-second world war document to deal explicitly with grammar was the secondary report of the Scottish Advisory Council on Education (1947) and it demonstrated a clear-thinking anti-traditional line on the place of grammar in schools. Barren exercises were condemned and their non-transfer to productive writing was asserted; teachers were to be free to decide how much grammar they needed and should be free of coercion in this decision (1947:229). Parsing and analysis as examination requirements were condemned; where grammar was taught it was to be functional and clearly related to pupils' writing and reading; error correction, that favourite practice of

25

nineteenth-century rhetoric, was dismissed as 'the grammar of what they (the pupils) never go wrong in' (1947:299).

The primary school document parallel with this report (1946) was a strong, clear memorandum which not only analysed the tradition of 'universal' grammar taught in schools but came firmly out against it. 'Grammar is not a primary means of learning correct English, but an apparatus of criticism; a formalisation of observed tendencies and usages into rules' (1946:236). 'We recommend (accordingly) that grammar should not be taught at all under that name in the earlier years of the primary school' (1946:237). The report recommended that teachers 'should throw away the crutches of interpretation and language exercises rather than have them become the boring grind of uninspired teaching' (1946:238).

If we compare with this highly reformatory document a contemporary syllabus in grammar for Edinburgh primary schools (1947) we find that grammar work was to last for five years, from 6+ to 11+, and its justification was this: '(It) is recognised that a certain knowledge of grammar is necessary to aid the correct speaking and writing of English. The pupils must be given standards to which errors may be referred' (1947:20). The scheme of work embraced a Latin-like parsing of noun, verb and 'all parts of speech', a knowledge by 10 years of age of clause analysis and by 11 of general analysis, together with certain etymological derivations. The inclusion of this last item under 'Grammar' is a curious indication of the nineteenth century origins of the scheme of work.

The contrast between the liberal recommendations of the report (1946) and the scheme of work (1947) serves to show (a) that the report was facing boldly a difficult and entrenched situation in the schools, and (b) that because of classroom inertia gross disparity might result between recommendations and classroom practice. It is interesting to note that the Edinburgh primary school syllabus panel, charged in 1965 with making a new scheme of work, opted out of making any grammatical prescriptions until linguistics pointed the way. Not only in Edinburgh, however, but elsewhere, liberalisation pressures, meeting well rooted traditional attitudes, may produce not reform but agnosticism.

We have noted the liberal tone of the report of the Advisory Council (1947) in its suggestions for secondary education. The 1952 memorandum on secondary English teaching was an illiberal force in its suggestions for writing and a reactionary and even damaging document in its dealings with grammar work in schools. It asserted that there were no solid grounds for the view that teaching traditional grammar was out of date or unnecessary (1952:21); grammar, sensibly taught, was an aid to correct expression; colloquial speech was inaccurate and incoherent and rendered recourse to teaching by appealing to the intuitions of the native speaker ineffective; pupils could only use *you and I* correctly if they knew the grammar of English dealing with subject, object, government and case form; knowledge of grammar would prevent such solecisms as *without me knowing*, *who* for *whom*, and *will be* for *shall be*; those who knew about the subjunctive would clear up the enigma of such phrases as *if I be* and *if I were*. The document pleaded with teachers to simplify their grammatical terminology, however, since an effective common nomenclature was necessary.

It is instructive to compare with this report (1952) contemporary provisions for the teaching of English language in English schools. The National Union of Teachers (1952) suggested no overt grammar work in secondary schools, although some incidental, *ad hoc* clearing up of points of usage is recommended. It is interesting to speculate whether the basic aims of English teaching in Scotland were the same as those for teaching the subject in England. The Ministry of Education pamphlet (1954) dealing specifically with language teaching in English implied that in *aim* no great disparity existed, and one would add that between provisions of the report of 1947 and the pamphlet of 1954 little methodological difference was suggested.

It is *Bulletin No. 1* of the Scottish Central Committee on English (1967) which confirms a progressive, liberal tone in new thinking about the syllabus in Scotland. In England, progressive post-war liberalisation might be seen from the Norwood Report (1943) onwards, although it could be argued that English attitudes to grammar were effectively revised from the second decade of this century. Scotland has only recently adopted a more open approach to language work and, because of its special cultural attitude to education referred to above, and discussed in Chapter 7, presents a problem of some magnitude for syllabus reformers. It would be a gross miscalculation to equate the uneasy shelving of the problem of grammar in the syllabus with any solution of the larger issues of the language syllabus.

In this atmosphere, *Bulletin No. 1* seemed to strike a bold new note for secondary schools, but, in its details, its language teaching recommendations represent merely a holding position. No overt language work of an analytic sort is proposed for the first stage of the secondary school (the common course). The second stage, that is, the first academic secondary stage, may follow the common course at the age of 11+ or 12+. The directives are merely these: grammar is to be incidental to textual study; rational discussion of points emerging is advocated; the pupil is to be helped to make critical assessment of writing, including his own; variety of language is urged as a main feature of language study and description useful in this area is called for. Finally, on the vexed question of terminology the document suggests that the syllabus '. . . requires that they (pupils) should gradually acquire a terminology sufficiently sophisticated to make it possible for them to talk adequately about language'.

This attitude to Scottish secondary work in English language is accompanied by some caveats about traditional school practices. The grammar/exercise book is to be abandoned. New grammar would not solve syllabus problems and, the Bulletin continued in a phrase of hopefulness, more detailed guidance on language teaching matters is awaited 'in the next few years' (1967:22).

At the time of going to press with this book the later bulletins of the Central Committee on English – particularly No. 5, which deals with language work – had just been published. However, first responses to *Bulletin No. 5* suggest that it will fulfil the hopes of more detailed guidance in language matters referred to in *Bulletin No. 1*. Nevertheless, there can be little doubt that an interesting and challenging situation may be detected in present day Scotland. In even the most anti-traditional documents there is a characteristic advocacy of rationalisation in the classroom, yet without any coherent rationale necessarily being available. Further, there is a desire to study language as a whole, but the teachers who advocate this seem not to have any clear idea of what this would imply for the syllabus.

It would appear that the problems of teaching English language in England are often similar to the Scottish case, especially where individual sectors of the school system, or regions of the country, have a tradition of rationalisation in their language work. The educational journals undoubtedly tend to stress the progressive aspect of reform, which is largely grammarless and is much taken up with creative writing programmes. At a practical school level, however, there is evidence that a very real sense of concern exists over the descriptive side of language work. It is very clear that the problems faced in London and the south of England, as they have been outlined in the publications of the Schools Council Research Programme on Linguistics and English Teaching impinge on the central issues we discuss in this book, although they have a different angle of attack.[2] The problems of English in Wales, which have a great many points linking them with the Scottish state of affairs, may be partly looked on as an issue for second language study but partly as a special case of second mother-tongue learning to which many of the discussions we raise would have relevance. It is hoped that the grammar debate we have outlined, together with the description of some of the problems met in Scotland, may not be wholly irrelevant to other parts of Britain.

## NOTES

[1] My attention was drawn to Andrews' work in 1964 by Mr. James Lochrie, Principal Lecturer in English at Jordanhill College of Education, when I was a lecturer on his staff.

[2] See Chapter 7, particularly note 4, where reference to *Language in Use* (1971) is made.

# 3 New Directions in Linguistics

Teachers who think about syllabus reform in English very often find themselves asking questions about academic linguistics. This is often a confusing experience since specialist teachers of English are almost always graduates with some experience of linguistic study in a British university and what they studied may not always seem relevant to their syllabus problem. Until about 1960, 'linguistic study' meant a study of the history and development of the English language. This might include a study of the grammar of Old English and of Middle English, together with translation and linguistic study of the texts of each period. According to the style of study in various universities, more or less comparative philology might be undertaken. In some centres students of English language might opt for detailed study of Old Norse or Old French, and various special papers exist for honours candidates in these fields and in others, including the study of modern English, that is English from about 1700 onwards.

During the thirties university interest in other fields of linguistic enquiry grew. In Britain, J. R. Firth, working closely with B. Malinowski the anthropologist, developed studies in sociolinguistics and in phonology and semantics which were much more in the tradition of Sweet – '. . . observing the phenomena of living languages' – than in the tradition of the nineteenth century German philology common in British universities during this period. In America, work was developing during the twenties and thirties in similar fields of anthropological linguistics with studies of American Indian languages by scholars such as Sapir. In the twenties and thirties in America, however, under the direction of Bloomfield and his followers, a whole new field of scientific linguistic study developed, sharply critical of much that was done in the name of language study both in the universities and in the schools. From linguists such as Firth and Bloomfield sprang a widespread and influential change of direction in university linguistic study, which we shall discuss in some detail in this chapter. The fruits of this change are to be seen in the present day status of linguistics in university study on both sides of the Atlantic. A remarkable development of interest in linguistic theory has overtaken us and has provided many universities with their fastest growth points of recent years.

The rise in interest in theoretical linguistics has triggered off a wide development in applied linguistics in universities and in colleges of education and other centres of language research. We have seen linguistics used extensively in courses for the re-training of teachers, in child language research and in studies of second and foreign language learning as well as in the description of the mother-tongue. Teachers have been faced with a vigorous fresh tradition of language study emanating from the universities and this has stimulated many to new kinds of enquiry into the problems of the school syllabus.

In the discussion which follows we shall try to sketch in three of the schools of thought which have taken part in this movement. We do so conscious of the need to simplify much of the field, or to stress particular aspects of linguistics for education. Not all that has been said by linguists is of interest to teachers of English; but even more important, not every teacher knows much of what the different schools of linguistics have said (and are still saying). It is thus with the double aim of informing and specifically briefing teachers of English that we present, under three headings, what is in fact a complex and rapidly growing (and changing) field of academic study.


## 3.1 The Influence of Bloomfield

The publication, in 1933, of Leonard Bloomfield's *Language* marks one of the most important events of the first fifty years of twentieth-century linguistics. This is true not only academically, since Bloomfield was an important theorist, but it is true of applications of linguistics also, because Bloomfield and his disciples have worked in many fields of applied linguistic enquiry, from the description of little known languages to the development of new techniques of native and foreign language teaching. Bloomfield's trenchant remarks on traditional school grammars, for example, set the tone for some thirty years of attack on school courses developed from formal grammars such as Poutsma (1914), Kruisinga (1917) and Jespersen (1928). This attack on accepted school grammars so effectively marks the work of Bloomfield and his followers that in some teachers' minds the

31

notion 'new linguistics' (a brash and worrying term) is wholly identified with criticism of existing school courses (see Chapter 4). This confusion, which has probably damaged school reform in English more than Bloomfield's revolutionary stimulus promoted it, is in itself reason enough for our further consideration of 'Bloomfieldianism'.

Bloomfield's scholarly position is not in debate here. From a historical point of view, few people would doubt the immense value and far reaching importance of his proposals. His *Language* was a work well attuned to its day (1933) and this can be seen in its proposals for a structural grammar which is closely linked with mechanistic behaviouristic psychology, characterised by scholars like Watson and later developed by Skinner. Bloomfield's analysis of language as a set of identifiable 'signals' described within a system of signals with little or no overt reliance on meaning in the analysis, is a strongly mechanistic study. It rejects a notional approach to language description, in which the meaning of an utterance may direct the grammatical description; it does not hold with functional approaches, and it is violently opposed to an 'idealistic' view of language where grammar is stated as a set of rules which prescribe the resources of the language system. Bloomfield advocated taking a sample of the language in use and subjecting it to a rigorous scientific analysis by means of identifying minimal units of the language's phonology and grammar and making a special kind of inventory of these items. His analysis of utterances usually proceeds by identifying the minimal elements of sentences and bracketing them together into structures (or trees) in such a way that smaller structures may be seen to be constituents of larger structures. His constituent analysis was a refreshing change of direction for linguistics from the semantically directed functional analysis of some traditional and most school grammars. Bloomfield preached a grammar of observed structures and he advocated study of a language by analysis of the distribution of the elements identified.

One would have expected a scholar of Bloomfield's stature to concern himself with theory alone and to leave questions of applications to his disciples, but in *Language*, Bloomfield repeatedly attacked school grammars and what he called the eighteenth century concepts which underlay them. At times his argument became extremely critical and, by European standards, showed intemperate antagonisms towards the traditional grammar used by the schools. For example, he held that school grammars

32

were fanciful and were based on the works of 'grammarians' (Bloomfield's quotes) (1933:496). He attacked schoolmasters who used these grammars, denouncing them as 'ignorant of linguistic science' and as people who 'wasted years of every child's life'; they were 'benighted' and 'authoritarian' and produced 'cultural inertia'. To many of us, these terms smack of emotional reaction and cloud the value of Bloomfield's contribution to the reform of the English language syllabus. Certainly, few linguists are willing to make this kind of attack today, and many scholars who followed Bloomfield closely in the thirties (and later) have subsequently softened their line on the denunciation of school grammars. Gleason, for example, the author of a standard 'Bloomfieldian' work of linguistics in 1955, said in 1964 that school grammars were often confused in teachers' minds with the traditional scholarly grammars from which they originally sprang. Thus, attacks on weakened school grammars might seem to some teachers to be attacks on the scholarship of Sweet or Jespersen, and *vice versa*. Academic debate arising from a question of scholarly grammar, Gleason argued, need not necessarily imply that all school courses following that grammar were corrupt, benighted and inefficient.

The tone of Bloomfield's attack may be traced in a wide field of American linguistic literature openly antagonistic to traditional school grammars of the parsing and sentence analysis sort. Fries, a contemporary of Bloomfield and author of the interesting but incomplete *American English Grammar* (1940) is one of the best known polemicists of the Bloomfieldian cause. His text *The Structure of English*, directed mainly to school teachers, represents the continuation of his work on the syntax of American English begun in his *Grammar*. It appeared in 1954 and profoundly influenced Roberts (*Patterns of English*, 1956) and others in their early courses offering 'new grammars' for schools.

The tone of intemperate claim and counter-claim which we have noted in Bloomfield, and can trace in Fries, continued in the fifties in that period of considerable upsurge in educational development which followed the launching of the first Russian *sputnik* in 1957. Scholars like Francis (1954) had spoken of 'a Darwinian-type revolution' sweeping through language study bringing a behaviouristic, synchronic, objective and scientific viewpoint into language description, and thus into schoolwork. Levin (1960) was still maintaining that traditional grammars such as those found in schools contained 'fallacies' which

33

he identified as *semantic* (they used notions of meaning to identify elements), *normative* (they prescribed rules for language use), and *logical* (their notions denied facts of distribution). In short Levin seems to see traditional grammarians as perversely unwilling to accept the gospel according to Bloomfield. As late as the mid-sixties, Roberts (1964, 1967) was maintaining that his position was anti-Latinate, anti-notional, speech-centred and anti-correctness in the authoritarian sense.

If we see these attacks, and the many lesser ones they stimulated at the level of articles in teachers' magazines and papers at educational conferences, etc., as part of a movement towards a new scientific viewpoint, positivist and empiricist, we can see linguistics-in-education running parallel to the physical sciences in its twentieth-century development. It is true that science embraced objective empirical approaches in the late nineteenth and early twentieth centuries under the influence of the positivist philosophers, and that the linguistics of Bloomfield followed suit only after a time lag of some forty years. Nevertheless, the two movements are closely linked. It was principally through contact with scientific method in psychology that Bloomfield was influenced. As we have hinted in our discussion, Bloomfield and his followers were over-enthusiastic about the behavioural approach and recent studies of the links between Bloomfieldianism and the psychology of the twenties (Watson, etc.) have suggested that Bloomfield was *plus royaliste que le roi*, and made excessive claims for the scientific method and behaviourism (see Lyons, 1970).

It is not surprising to find that teachers have in many places reacted against the over-stated case of Bloomfield and have moved back to traditional grammar in their work, or have rejected Bloomfield as an unsatisfactory last ditch position within grammar. One feels that, had Chomsky not firmly reasserted his faith in the underlying philosophy of traditional grammar, a state of anarchy worse than the authoritarianism of old traditional courses might have prevailed in the language classroom. As it is, Chomsky, Halliday, Lyons, Lamb and others have presented theoretical viewpoints which reassert the notional basis of grammar and reject Bloomfield's mechanistic structuralism on scholarly grounds. It is this movement which seems to have restored a measure of balance to the debate on school grammars.

Two rather serious issues have been noted in the classroom as the result of Bloomfield's assertions and their subsequent rejection by scholarship. Bloomfield and his disciples very

34

effectively fixed in teachers' minds that linguistics for application to school courses essentially meant 'structuralism'. A new authoritarianism sprang up; old faiths were re-committed to new gods. But teachers who were wooed and won by the new orthodoxy were no sooner confirmed in their belief than they found it attacked, undermined and virtually refuted by Chomsky. It is obvious that considerable confusion has resulted from this. Some teachers have expressed dismay; others have pleaded for guidance. While it is sad that good should have to come out of disappointment, it is probably true to argue that the rejection of Bloomfield has reminded teachers that it is never wise to be so partisan in education. It has asserted the need for a cautious eclecticism in all our approaches to theory, particularly theory dealing with the nature of language and language learning. The rejection of structuralism as a panacea may have been a chastening experience for some, but has produced an excellent climate for real reform of the language syllabus.

The schools of America and to a lesser extent of Britain were greatly stirred up by the structuralists, particularly Fries. Many curricular reform projects were set in hand, and some of them have modified their proposals in tune with the later diminution of interest in structuralism. Most valuable of all results from this whole movement was a spirit of self-examination in teaching circles which has opened many doors for further reforms. In the spirit of eclectics, then, we ought to consider some of the specific points made by structuralists which stirred teachers during the fifties and sixties. Many of them may still have a therapeutic effect.

Nida (1960) in a published version of a 1943 thesis, presents us with a careful account of the position of structuralism *vis-à-vis* traditional scholarly grammars – perhaps the best discussion of the principles of constituent analysis we have before Postal (1964). He criticises traditional grammar for its lack of a category of *order* in its syntax, pointing out that only unusual word order was dealt with by the major grammarians. Thus grammarians might go out of their way to show that 'Seldom (have I seen) . . .' involves unusual inversion of subject and verb in the declarative. 'Bread have I and to spare' and similar literary forms might fall under discussion, but no theory of normal syntactic order is proposed by traditional grammars. This, in our view, touches on the important and long-standing point that school grammars have often found it very difficult to decide whether word order involved questions of grammar or questions of style. In recent years mainly through the work of Halliday (1967a, e, etc.) much more attention has been paid to this question.

One of Nida's pleas was for a proper taxonomy to be developed in grammar, that is, a properly defined relationship between meaning, form and substance, and within each area, for a proper identification of elements which make its analysis possible. This plea links effectively with a long felt need of education to think more clearly about *aspects* or *levels* of analysis. Firth and Halliday, and many others in European linguistics, have made similar proposals and we shall consider them in due course. But from a practical teaching or textbook writing point of view, discrimination of levels is very valuable; traditional language work in schools tended to distinguish subjects to be taught (orthography, reading, grammar, etc.) rather than the aspects of language description giving rise to them.

Finally, Nida (and several of his associates including Fries and Roberts) associated himself with a revision of grammatical terminology. He was particularly interested in revising the meaning-based terms of traditional grammar like the names for some parts of speech, e.g. *noun*, and some functions of elements of syntax, like *subordinate*. He was aware that a strong authoritarianism was associated with the terminology of traditional grammar and he pointed to a self-perpetuating situation, affecting teachers largely, in which the traditional terminology of grammar fostered an authoritarian point of view in the teaching of languages, which in turn promoted a demand for the terminology. Further, most traditional courses in schools concentrated on written texts and on formal styles; thus, a restricted rhetorical range contributed to a limited grammatical attitude.

There is little doubt that Nida and his colleagues raised points of considerable importance for teachers today. His tone is calm and his style scholarly — in sharp contrast with much of the debate by structuralists and others who have taken their style from Bloomfield. Teachers who find themselves interested in the traditional-versus-structural debate could give themselves no better briefing than Nida's *Synopsis* (1960) which has recently been made available (1966) in a new edition.

The text most teachers will know best from the structuralist camp is Fries's *The Structure of English* (1954). In effect it is a late chapter of his *American English Grammar* — the chapter on syntax — which appeared fourteen years after the grammar itself (1940). *Structure* was produced for an applying audience, not a theoretical one, and one cannot fail to notice what a strong appeal to education the text has. Fries attacked the conceptual basis of grammatical terminology and of the formal operations of traditional grammar, rather as Nida had done. His discussion of the definition of 'sentence' brought together a large number of existing textbook definitions, all of which were condemned as notional or mentalist.

Fries saw the sentence through Bloomfield's eyes as a series of hierarchically related constituents, that is, each identifiable structure could be seen as consisting of two identifiable lesser constituents (occasionally more than two). Constituents could be broken down, or bracketed, until the lowest grammatically meaningful element of structure was reached. Fries showed that form classes could be derived from the items identified in this way, but he argued that his form classes were not 'parts of speech', but distributionally significant elements of structure which we can identify by structural signals. His slot-and-filler (or pattern) approach to language exercises is based on this.

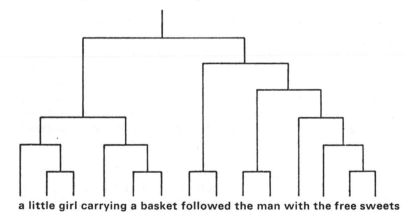

**a little girl carrying a basket followed the man with the free sweets**

This form of analysis is related to the traditional subject–predicate approach, but it is much more detailed. It introduces, for example, the *level* at which certain elements are separated. Further, it relates elements, such as prepositional phrases, to the sentence in an explicit way. In its essence this form of analysis is a bracketing operation, although we have adopted the 'tree' as our explanatory aid here.

Reviewers saw Fries's *Structure* as an exciting book for education and for linguistics, although several reviews noted that it was deficient in its phonology (see Sledd, 1955). Sledd noted a 'gaudy contradiction' in Fries's standpoint. If only structural signals could be relevant to phonology and grammar, how can an utterance ever be recognised? Unless we know that the sounds we are hearing are part of, say, an intelligible series of utterances over the telephone, how can we even begin our analysis? To Sledd, the exclusion of all 'mentalist' considerations in language analysis was contradictory and misleading. He seemed not to accept Fries's statement in 1954 that 'same' and 'different' were all that one needed in a semantic theory underlying recognition.

Fries strongly influenced Roberts (1956) and many less-well-known textbook writers. His influence can be traced in Britain in the discussions of Quirk (1959, 1962), in Strang (1962), in Mittins (1959, 1962) and Whitehall (1968) and in many lesser writers. Roberts' (1956) *Patterns of English* was used along with Fries's *Structure* in several colleges of education in Britain and in a few schools. One Edinburgh school at least was still using Roberts' *Patterns* in 1969 as a senior language study book.

In a survey in the *Linguistic Reporter*, Kreidler (1966) analysed thirty school textbooks with avowed 'linguistic' components. Only three authors used post-Bloomfieldian approaches in their analysis of English, even at this late date. Most of the texts were largely concerned with constituent analysis in the style of Fries and Bloomfield. Only one textbook in the sample, taken from American school lists, dealt with phonology.

Kreidler's survey, over thirty years after Bloomfield's main book, shows that American mother-tongue education at least has been considerably influenced by structuralism. While a survey of British textbooks of the same period would have shown both a wider range of linguistic affiliation and a more independent exposition of the theory behind each course, there can be little doubt that structuralism would also appear as a significant line of approach. It appears in a particularly clear way in the general notions of 'language' and 'linguistics' which have begun to appear in progressive discussions of educational method, in course syllabuses and in conference and training programmes for teachers. Whitehead, writing in 1966, referred to Fries (1952) and Roberts (1956) as if they were the principal sources of linguistic reform for education. Flower (1966) in a sagely argued chapter on grammar in the schools of Britain looked for 'a new functional, structural grammar' and wrote extensively about Fries's contribution, even if at the same time he paid Chomsky lip service (mis-naming him 'Nicholas') and advocating (most acceptably) a careful study of the whole field of language in education before we committed ourselves to classroom grammar at all.

It must be clear to any teacher who studies the effects of structuralism on education that a considerable liberating stimulus derived initially from Bloomfield and his followers. It is equally clear that many sins were committed in the name of this liberty. A new dogmatism arose from the jaunty attacks structuralism made on the establishment; a mechanistic view of both language and learning was foisted on teachers. It is very much to be regretted that this has, in recent years, largely obscured the value that fresh thinking about distribution, structure, element definition and labelling has had for syllabus reform. Certainly, we would not want teachers to become structuralists, but every well-trained teacher of English should be able to manipulate the constituent analysis proposed by structuralists. We do not want meaningless analysis in the classroom, but we cannot lose by having our teachers' awareness of the physical signals of language sharpened. Above all, Bloomfield, Fries and Roberts are excellent authors for teachers to study and exercise their critical judgement on in the light of practical classroom problems.

## 3.2 M. A. K. Halliday and Firthian Linguistics

The main impact of modern linguistics on British educational thought did not take place until the early sixties of this century although a distinguished line of linguistic scholarship particular to Britain existed from Sweet in the nineteenth century through Firth in the 1930s and 1940s up to the present day. It might be argued that this slightly later burgeoning of school interest in linguistics was a blessing; most of the crude classroom applications of structuralism in America took place in the 1950s. British education, however, has maintained a more even view of its classroom needs than has been evidenced in America. There has been a stronger sense of tradition in British education; there has been less prescription of syllabus directions by state and other authorities; most important, there has been a degree of independence of university educationists and linguists shown in Britain which has not been matched in America.

In the last decade, however, the work of linguists of British universities has considerably influenced syllabus research and reform. Outstanding among these linguists have been Halliday, Quirk, McIntosh, Abercrombie, Strevens, Sinclair and others whose papers have been read at teachers' conferences and whose articles and books form the basis of much specialist training and re-training conducted in the Colleges of Education.[1] While these scholars are by no means all the names concerned, and further, while their books and papers represent only a *stage* in the statement of a linguistic viewpoint which has developed rapidly since the early sixties, historically speaking their books and the attitudes they promoted have set the direction of much influential work in education, including research and textbook writing.

Halliday's *Categories* (1961) was widely read and discussed by teachers in England and Scotland, although it was principally in Scotland that the early study and applications of this work were undertaken. This paper set out an early approach to systemic grammar (often called 'scale and category grammar' in its early years). Fundamentally, a systemic grammar is concerned with the networks of systems, or choice options, which could be said to underlie an utterance. On the one hand we have an observed text (or a text which could have been spoken appropriately by a native speaker) and on the other we have a rationalisation of what might be said to be its underlying grammar in terms of the path through grammar systems such as transitivity, mood and theme by which the utterance is realised. When we look at a written text, or listen to a spoken one – examining its surface, as it were, (which is *one* stratum of text) we have observable series of elements. We could bracket these elements, label them and make numerous analyses of them at will. For example, we could note 'noun + verb + noun' in a clause. But at a deeper level of grammar we could discover relationships, dependencies and the functionally important bonds between elements which encode speaker meaning and attitude. All of these relationships, deep down in the grammar, are in systems of choices available to the user. Taken far enough, this can become a sociolinguistic operation. Under an observed utterance lie networks of choices –

the grammar systems of the language; behind or prior to these we might describe the network of relationships which exist in society which in turn give rise to the need to steer an utterance through appropriate channels of dependencies to be realised at the surface as a meaningful, effective sentence, clause, phrase, etc. Thus, Halliday in his systemic approach is concerned with strata of analysis, one of which – the surface – is much more concerned with structural issues, such as labelling, and bracketing, than the others below. *Categories* (1961) concerned itself more with the approach to the surface utterance than with the underlying grammar systems, although the paper mentions systems (it is one of the categories) and sketches in its role in the analysis of text. We shall discuss this below.

Halliday is Firth's interpreter and apologist, particularly in two fields; firstly, in grammar (and its systems) and secondly, in the important relationships distinguishable between language utterances and their social and stylistic contexts. We have already noted that Firth was sociologically orientated in much of his linguistic work. He and Malinowski, the anthropologist, worked closely together in London in the thirties. In semantics Firth's approach was a contextual one (meanings in contexts) closely related to anthropological interests where utterances and the circumstances in which the language is uttered form the pillars of the study. In his grammar and phonology, Firth operated firmly from a basis of the meaningfulness of texts; all linguistic statements, he claimed, were statements of meaning. His view of 'meaning' was that a semantic theory should be sufficiently wide to embrace all formal aspects of the grammar of a language, its lexis and its phonology and his view of language-in-context was that all relevant aspects of the non-language situation (participants, place, attitude, etc.) should be considered relevant to the analysis. It was in his development of the idea of 'context of situation' that Firth made his main contribution to European linguistics.[2] He offered us strikingly little on syntax. In one sense, then, Halliday's work complements Firth's by contributing an approach to syntax and grammar system lacking in Firth. In another light, however, Halliday has developed with great originality, lines of thought little more than mentioned by Firth, for example in studies of intonation, and the thematic organisation of language, some of his views on which we shall discuss below. Teachers who would like an introductory general view to Firth's work should read his *Tongues of Men* (1937) produced recently as a paperback together with *Speech* in 1964.

Firth has been noted as a strong proponent of the idea that analytic concepts exist only within the descriptive system of the linguist and not in the language itself. In Allen's terms 'There are no facts in linguistics until the linguist has made them; they are ultimately like all scientific facts, the products of imagination and invention' (1957). Thus, there were no theoretical difficulties for Firth in identifying conceptual and organisational systems serving different aspects of language analysis. Halliday has made the most important statement to date on this question of 'aspects' in his approach to the levels of language analysis, discussed in the opening stages of his *Categories* (1961) and in several other places including Halliday, McIntosh and Strevens (1964b). He identifies a level of *substance* (the aspect of analysis concerned with the raw material – phonic and graphic – of language), *form* (the aspect dealing with the organisation of grammar and lexis) and *situation* (the aspect of language study dealing with the extra-textual features of utterance). A link between substance and form gives us *phonology* and *graphology* (or *orthography*); and a parallel link between form and situation gives us *context*. Most exponents of the idea of 'levels of analysis' use the broader term 'semantics' for the link between form and situation, retaining the term 'context' as one class of relationship within semantics.

**Chart of Levels, taken from Halliday (1961) (Slightly adapted)**

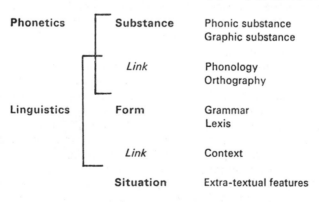

| Phonetics | Substance | Phonic substance<br>Graphic substance |
| | *Link* | Phonology<br>Orthography |
| Linguistics | Form | Grammar<br>Lexis |
| | *Link* | Context |
| | Situation | Extra-textual features |

Under this view of 'levels' a highly abstract and broad spectrum of linguistic activity may be embraced. Aspects of language

42

study ranging from the physical properties of sound or the perceived qualities of patterns of marks to questions of form and meaning may be studied in a broad, unified approach to utterance.

Halliday's *Categories* (1961) proposed four theoretical concepts which ought to lie behind the description of a human language. Three of them were categories relating to the observed structure of language and the fourth related to underlying systems of language. While Hallidean theory and its applications have moved considerably from this early position, it is important for us to remember two things about *Categories*: firstly, Halliday has developed several of the concepts of this paper into the much more elaborate systemic grammar he now proposes; secondly, in their 1961 form Halliday's proposals had a wide and stimulating effect on educational thought.

The basic tenet of the 1961 paper is that language is patterned human activity and that careful observation of a given language can show stretches of that language which carry recurring patterns. These identifiable stretches of language exemplify the category *unit* of language. In most languages these units can be seen to form a special kind of hierarchy arranged from highest to lowest. Thus, English shows a hierarchy of sentence, clause, group (or phrase), word and morpheme. This hierarchy is called the *rank scale* of units and it offers us a useful formal device for identifying and defining units, since it is a taxonomy in which each higher rank is made up of one or more of the units of the rank next below. That is, sentence is made up of one or more clauses; clause is made up of one or more phrases, etc. This useful identification of units and rank embraces the traditional notion of higher and lower grammatical units, but it also stresses the need for these units to be more carefully identified. In traditional grammar there was a tendency for the unit *sentence* to be identified (although the semantic definition produced problems) and for clauses, phrases and words to be lumped together under the general notion of *words*. In Halliday's view a scale of only two ranks was inadequate for English. In proposing a five rank hierarchy for English he mentioned the possibility that a higher unit, the paragraph, might one day be added to the scale, but that at present we have no grammar of the paragraph in any accepted sense.

The notion of rank carried with it the idea of rank-shift. If a structurally identifiable clause enters into the structure of a sentence we would say that the 'home' position of the rank scale had been demonstrated. Thus a main clause and an adjective clause might together make up a sentence. If, however, an adjective clause were found to be embedded in, say, a noun phrase, it could be held to be *rank-shifted*, e.g. *The sailors who had lifebelts were saved*. The clause 'who had lifebelts' is clearly defining, and is part of the subject noun phrase 'The sailors'. Phonologically it merges with the subject phrase, and is in phonological and grammatical contrast with *The sailors, who had lifebelts, were saved*. In further confirmation of the difference of status of the adjective clauses in the sentences quoted, each is semantically different. In the first example (the embedded defining clause) it is clear that some sailors were not saved, or at least there is this very strong implication; in the second case (the 'nested' non-defining clause) we are led to believe that all the sailors were saved because they had lifebelts. Gleason (1965) points out, as many other scholars do, that the non-defining adjective clause is probably not an adjective clause at all, but rather like a second principal clause 'and they had lifebelts'. This and other problems arise from a consideration of the rank scale. Matthews (1966), for instance, found that the rank scale encouraged the view that everything was rank-shifted and thus rendered itself invalid. Halliday's reply (1966c), contained in the same journal, shows that Matthews was thinking of rank-shift in terms of a phrase-structure grammar, whereas he proposed that there was a distinction between morphological types of structure and functions associated with them. Halliday maintains that a notion of rank where *x* can function as *y* is illuminating. In this he would seem to have the support of educationists, and the backing of traditional grammar.

If units are the stretches of language which carry observable patterns we need a category to deal with the patterns themselves. This is provided for in the second of Halliday's categories, *structure*. At the surface of language one can identify and label elements. Further, one can bracket these elements together in certain ways consistent with the theory and show that structure is a question of elements in places. The idea of a progression of elements in language gives us the notion of sequence, and identifies the still more important issue of order in syntax. It was from this part of Halliday's proposals that teachers drew what has been crudely called the SPCA approach to clause structure. The symbols, proposed in *Categories* might be glossed as S 'subject place'; P 'predicator place'; C 'complement place'; A 'adjunct place'. This view of elements in places has been used quite extensively by teachers in the classroom, as May (1967) and

Currie (1967), and, in New Zealand, by Scott *et al.* (1968), and a considerable range of unpublished classroom materials, show. In itself, it is an interesting, limited analysis of the 'many I-C's' type, – that is, in contrast with Bloomfield's constituent analysis in which there was binary division of sentences and all subsequent parts until the minimal unit of structure was reached (the morpheme). Hudson has put it like this: 'The first group (few IC's) segments the clause itself into a relatively small number of immediate constituents, but requires a relatively large number of further segmentations before the ultimate constituents are reached, each segmentation yielding a further layer of structure. The second group of grammars (many IC's) segments the clause into a relatively large number of immediate constituents, each of which then requires a relatively small number of segmentations before the ultimate constituents are reached' (1967:1). He illustrates the difference by using the sentence *John has paid ten pounds for his ticket*. (See the next page.)

It will be noticed that the second of these analyses identifies a series of elements in a sequence. This might be called a simple structural labelling process. The places these occupy were called S, P, C and A respectively in 1961. The arguments in favour of retaining at least the surface identification of these four elements in their sequence in an English clause are that it is simpler than the few IC's approach typified by phrase-structure grammars *à la* Chomsky, that it is more resourceful than the few IC's approach since it forms the basis of a systemic grammar, and that the phrase-structure model, part of a transformational generative grammar, is neither necessary nor sufficient for clause analysis, while the simpler many IC's approach can reveal surface order, element function and underlying systems of grammar as part of an integrated description of the language (Hudson, 1967). These claims are powerful and very probably just. Systemic grammar is, however, by no means fully formed and much interesting work is in hand. Ten years of schoolwork, however, does lend practical support to the claim that the many IC's model (based on Halliday, 1961) is simple to use in class, can lead on to much more profound statements about language than mere identification of elements in places; it can also form part of a functional approach to language, which has always received the support of education.

In this discussion of analysis, we have already illustrated the third of Halliday's 1961 categories, *class*. At the surface of language, when we segment a structure we can group similar

**Few IC's Analysis (after Chomsky) 1965:**

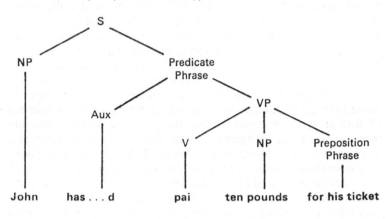

**Many IC's Analysis ( after Halliday):**

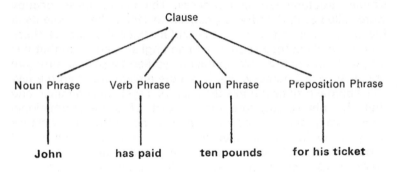

events together. Thus noun phrases, verb phrases, prepositional phrases, can be labelled. This is classification of item. It names the elements in the chain of elements which makes up part of the syntagm of the language. In one sense this is a very valuable part of any grammar since class label gives us a hand-hold on form which is not also a statement of function. Statements of function can subsequently be made. Therefore, in rank-shift we can say class of item X functions as Y. Traditional grammar classified in this way, but in many school grammars the distinction between class and function was blurred by sentences being

46

described as consisting of a subject phrase and a finite verb. 'Subject' is a syntactic function; 'finite verb' is a grammatical class. In the interests of effective description, this distinction should be kept clear.

We have discussed three categories proposed by Halliday in his 1961 paper, *unit, structure* and *class*. In our presentation of these three categories we have looked forward from Halliday's 1961 position into what has several times been referred to as a 'systemic' grammar. In fact the elements of systemic grammar were stated in 1961 when Halliday proposed as his fourth category, *system*. System was presented as a very different kind of category from the more structurally orientated unit, structure and class, which preceded it. It was defined as the finite range of mutually exclusive and mutually defining choices which underlie the selection of an item in structure. Broadly, system answers the question 'Why choose that form rather than another in the realisation of an utterance?' It is from this notion of underlying systems and surface realisations that Halliday's 'deep' and 'surface' grammar has been developed since 1964.

In simple diagrammatic form proposals for a systemic grammar look like this:

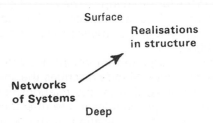

This is sometimes called a 'realisation' grammar since it concerns itself with the realisation of dependencies and other relationships selected by the underlying grammar. In a sense this kind of grammar fulfils one of the definitions of a transformational grammar, in that there is a link between deep and surface analyses. However, this is the weakest definition of 'transformational' possible and is probably better abandoned. True transformational grammar proposes elaborate rules to adjust the symbols of base strings to output strings. Halliday has not yet done this, nor, perhaps, would he want to. He simply uses the notion of realisation at this stage in developing a systemic

47

grammar (1966b) and later the term 'a realisation statement' which was attached to a systemic statement, and which proposed the structure (or structures) of the output of the grammar. Structure is therefore predictable when the underlying systemic networks have directed the choices.

The structural functions and the intonational features of a unit can therefore be seen as the realisations of options. Options of what sort? The systems having the clause as their point of origin are three — *transitivity*, *mood* and *theme*. These terms formalise three areas which it might be useful to discuss briefly in this chapter since the concepts, if not the details of the approach, are already in use in English teaching.

*Transitivity* deals with the effect of the action of the verb on the external world. Sometimes transitivity is called the 'semantic' function of the clause because it informs us of 'the factual, objective content of extralinguistic reality' (Bühler, in Halliday, 1969). It deals with questions of who or what is the process, the actor and the goal. For example, in the clause 'The old man is eating cake' 'is eating' is the *process*, 'the old man' is the *actor*, and 'cake' is the *goal*. In finer detail, the networks of options in transitivity also deal with processes like directed and non-directed action on a goal, and 'ascription' in which an attribute is ascribed to an actor, as in 'he looked happy'. The kind of clause which will be realised at the surface will reflect the functions appropriate to the objective content of the process and its actor (see Halliday, (1967e, f, 1968a)).

Transitivity is a large and important network of the clause, but it is not the only one. *Mood* prescribes the so-called 'speech functions' of the clause, that is, the relationships between the participants and their speech roles in the utterance. For example the imperative form is the realisation of the relationship of the speaker ordering someone to do something; the interrogative reflects someone asking for something. Traditional grammar viewed mood in this way by specifying an informal set of relationships which were satisfied by certain forms of the language. It is interesting to note, however, that Halliday's systemic proposals are, in mood and theme, which we will discuss below, close to aspects of rhetoric. Mood is a characterisation of the influences speakers bring to bear on their hearers, of persuasion, and intention. It is capable of subtleties such as the question asked as part of a yes—no sequence, which reaches out to discourse grammar, because it goes beyond the clause and its systems; it is concerned with the question which makes a state-

48

ment requiring no answer although in wh- form, – the so-called 'rhetorical' question. Speaker role clearly embraces considerations of speaker intention. No formalisation of this set of options has yet been made, but there is obviously a very important field defined by systems of mood which link together several of the issues in language teaching discussed elsewhere in this book.

*Theme* has been described as the structure of communication in terms of its messages, their distribution and the information carried by them. It is a system of options embracing such notions as 'given' and 'new' information, or as some have identified it, as *theme* and *rheme*. Information carried by a clause is carried by the grammatical structure, obviously, but equally importantly, it is also marked by the intonation of the clause. We know that we can alter the information carried in a clause by changing the stress:

*I* didn't go to the theatre;
I didn't go to the *theatre*.

Points of prominence in the language help us to identify what Halliday has described as information units (1967b), or more informally, 'message blocks'. This organisation of messages is not effectively described by syntax, but needs a sensitive intonational system to describe it effectively. Halliday has repeatedly asserted that there are certain patterns of linguistic organisation expounded by intonation, just as there are others expounded by grammar. But they are not mutually exclusive. Many grammatical options indicating mood, for instance, are also intonationally marked, as part of the great redundancy of information signals language contains. The notion of systems of theme explores the underlying options of marked or unmarked information in clauses realised in the output by certain identifiable linguistic features.

Halliday's effects on the teaching of English in schools have, in our opinion, been far reaching and important. They had an early phase in which teachers rather too enthusiastically prepared 'new grammars' for their classes using the first three of the categories from the 1961 paper. Many appeared to believe that a simple SPCA bracketing of clause elements on the one hand solved the long-standing problems of general analysis in the syllabus and on the other fairly reflected the proposals of Halliday. As usual, there is an important half-truth in the use of SPCA analysis. It does represent a more manipulable and potentially more useful mode of clause analysis, but only when it is seen as a

| The grocer | lifted | the box | from the car |
|------------|--------|---------|--------------|
| S | P | C | A |

part – a basic but minor part – of a complete language description which, as we have shown, is by no means completed yet. On balance, one feels that the hasty introduction of surface bracketing had a good effect. Certainly, it disappointed teachers who were expecting some kind of panacea for the ills of the syllabus; assuredly, it led to a form of crude authoritarianism at times, 'new presbyter is old priest writ large'; but equally clearly, it stimulated a widespread and continuing interest in the organisation of language – a phenomenon which had not really been noted in schools in Britain since the affair of the Report of the Joint Committee on Grammatical Terminology (1911) and its immediate aftermath, discussed in Chapter 2.

The little grammars which teachers produced on the Hallidean pattern were often quite interesting. May's 'Glasgow Grammar' (1967) was produced by a committee of teachers who worked for two years to interpret Halliday's 1961 grammar for the schools. When this booklet was published some of the teachers concerned rather regretted having gone into print and 'crystallised' their proposals when Halliday and the world of linguistic theory in general were in dynamic flux. Here again, on balance I believe publication to have been a good thing. Naturally Scottish teachers are going to be wary of the next grammar, and the next, and in the end they may even decide that they are not in the market for grammars at all in syllabus reform. But the maturity which is now being shown has undoubtedly stemmed from practical experience of recent years.

Currie (1967) and (1969), the first two books published in the *Discovering Language* series, tried to present a wider view of language, its patterns and its varieties than had been common in teachers' *ad hoc* courses. Both books embraced aspects of surface structure, and aspects of systemic organisation in their description; both were much inspired by Halliday's work from 1961 to 1967. Neither book purported to be a grammar, although grammar is fairly widely discussed as one of the aspects of language. Further, throughout the course (now completed)

50

there is a studied eclecticism. Halliday's ideas are latent in the work rather than the content of it.

The publications of the Schools Council Programme 'Linguistics and English Teaching' show a wide area in which Halliday's ideas have been influential. He was the director of the project and its driving force. The team of the project has produced ten papers for teacher guidance and a bibliography, covering topics ranging from the teaching of reading and writing in schools to linguistic aspects of cohesion in the English clause. Independent of this the team has produced a wide range of experimental classroom materials, *Language in Use* (1971), published by the Schools Council. These materials, designed for general secondary school use rather than for selective courses, or specialised groups, represent an important statement of attitude to syllabus reform. Linguistics plays the part of informing the teachers – an inspirational role, one might say – but there are remarkably few instances in the lessons where one is conscious of intrusion.

Halliday himself has written about applications of linguistics in school programmes. Perhaps his best known contribution is in *The Linguistic Sciences and Language Teaching* (1964b) when with McIntosh and Strevens he produced the first real teaching statement of the impact of linguistics on language teaching. The book was influential, was well received and is still studied. But it could be argued that it was out of date when it first appeared. In 1962 substantial portions of this book were read in manuscript by Scottish teachers. When the book appeared in 1964 it was becoming clear that the growth of transformational generative linguistics and the development of the systemic side of Halliday's own theory were of enough moment to make the statement of the 1964 book of limited value at best. In a sense Sinclair's grammar (1965) suffered the same fate. Events in linguistic theory move with such rapidity that the time lag of publication may be disastrous. It seems to me that both books mentioned above are now more valuable than they were. The position *SHAM* indicated *vis-à-vis* methodology and linguistics is a fascinating one, something students and teachers should study carefully. Sinclair's 1965 grammar is a splendid statement of the structural part of a systemic grammar.[3]

Indirectly, Halliday's papers delivered to teachers' conferences and study groups form an important mode of contact between linguistics and education. Sadly, much of this material was never published, and as is usual with study group work, the direction and scope of the discussions which followed these papers has not been preserved. Several points from these papers appear in this book, but one cannot claim to have represented even a fraction of the content or response involved.[4]

There can be little doubt that Hallidean ideas constitute one of the significant influences of our time on British education. Bloomfield took a destructive and even a vicious attitude to school language work; Chomsky has been marked by a studied agnosticism on the question of applications. Halliday has maintained a steady and fruitful contact with educational programmes for over a decade. He has done this not only through his contact with the Schools Council but through teachers and lecturers whom he has influenced. In this one feels that the interest of Firth in British education has been continued in Halliday, and it is our view that this interest is in a fruitful and developing state today.

## NOTES

[1]   Specially important in this sphere have been M. A. K. Halliday's 1961 paper *Categories of the Theory of Grammar*, Barbara Strang's *Modern English Structure* (1962), John Sinclair's *Edinburgh Course of Spoken English: Grammar* (1965) and Halliday, McIntosh and Strevens' book *The Linguistic Sciences and Language Teaching* (1964). The last work is widely known by its nickname *SHAM*.

[2]   Firth's contribution to European linguistics also includes the development of 'prosodic' phonology, but since this has not significantly affected English teaching we do not discuss it here.

[3]   Since writing this, John Sinclair's *A Course in Spoken English: Grammar* (1972) has come into my hands in proof form. It is a much more detailed work than (1965) and constitutes a very important statement of the principles of a systemic grammar.

[4]   A forthcoming work in Oxford University Press's *LALL* (*Language and Language Learning*) series by Gunter Kress is to publish a selection of readings from Halliday's work, together with commentary.

## 3.3 Transformational Generative Linguistics and School Grammars

The publication of Chomsky's *Syntactic Structures* in 1957 marked one of the most important theoretical events of twentieth-century linguistics. It was the first main statement of what has become known as transformational generative linguistics (TG

52

for short). It was the earliest of a series of statements couched in mathematico-logical terms of a rationalist position which 'correctly' characterised the sentences of a language. Teachers and others might find the term 'correct' a little misleading. It means in this context, 'consistent', maximally explicable by the theory, or, to be slightly cynical, able to explain a structure in TG terms in such a way that other TG grammarians could not propose a better characterisation. *Syntactic Structures* proposed an outline of a device (in the sense of a logical method) which was expressed as a series of propositions and rules, which purported to be able to account for all the acceptable sentences of a language (and *only* the acceptable ones). In technical terms the device 'generates' their grammar in a formally acceptable set of equations. Under this approach, which has now become a world-wide basis of grammatical study, grammarians are, more and more, taken up with writing the logical rules which will give as their output (or 'derive') a set of symbols which can be converted into the sentence itself.

Perhaps the most important thing to note at this point, for our particular educational approach, is that Chomsky significantly moved away from the study of language as a corpus of utterances with physically identifiable language signals which we would, like Bloomfield, label and bracket to form our linguistic analysis. Bloomfield and the structuralists were 'corpus-centred' in their approach; Chomsky is 'model-centred' in his. The task of the theoretical linguist is to devise models of language and justify them within the logical and mathematical sciences. Chomsky has put it like this:

'. . . the problem for linguistic theory is to discover general properties of any system of rules that may serve as the basis for a human language, that is, to elaborate in detail what we may call, in traditional terms, the general *form of language* that underlies each particular realisation, each particular natural language.' (1966a : 10) (Chomsky's italics)

Chomsky's proposals for a rationalist grammar should be thought of as an achievement of theory — possibly the most significant theoretical proposal since de Saussure — and not as a ready-made proposal for educational practice. Yet, a considerable effect on language teaching may be traced, particularly in America, despite the fact that Chomsky's 1957 proposals underwent important changes in the first decade of their reign. It would be true to say that while many British teachers know about TG and are orientated by it in some of their problem areas (e.g. child language acquisition; psycholinguistics) no extensive applications of TG in classroom courses have yet appeared in Britain. In America, as Kreidler (1966) notes in his excellent survey, there have been two different categories of applications of TG in schoolwork. Firstly, some writers distinguish the basic ideas of TG and introduce them as interesting theoretical ideas to teachers. Secondly, some writers make actual use of the TG model with its strings of symbols and rules. He lists three texts by Roberts (1962, 1964, 1966–67) and two by other writers which exemplify this kind of direct application.

A close study of Roberts' *English Sentences* (1962) shows the book to be a bridge between structuralist concepts and transformational ones. It was Roberts' first text after Chomsky (1957); all his previous work had been profoundly influenced by Bloomfield and Fries in grammar and Trager and Smith in phonology. Roberts (1962) is an amalgam of Fries (1952), Trager and Smith (1951) and Chomsky (1957). That is, a simple structuralist analysis based on the bracketing together of the structural elements of sentences beginning with the spoken language and regarding the written language as some kind of weak imitation of speech. It would seem that Roberts regarded Chomsky's proposals as a way of analysing text – virtually as a way of carrying out the kind of operations school analysis might demand – subject/predicate, extensions of predicate, etc. He thus misdescribes Chomsky's P-rules (that part of Chomsky's grammar which accounts for basic constituent analysis) as a method of carrying out a grammatical description. But they are not this; they are part of a larger grammatical operation related to the entire TG rule system. Structuralists envisaged a phrase structure grammar as a way of bracketing sentences and revealing their structure; TG grammarians regard their P-rules as an analysis of base strings which gives output symbols which subsequently are processed through transformation rules and phonological output rules (and, if possible, also semantic rules) to reach the level of utterance.

Roberts further interprets the transformational rules of Chomsky as simple rules for the conversion of existing sentences into other forms. Thus he 'transforms' active into passive by a rule altering the positions of subject and object and changing the verb to its appropriate passive form. In TG the T-rules adjust base string symbols to output symbols. That is, it is an operation within a calculus of rules, meaningful only as a theoretical step within the mathematics of the grammar; it is *not* manipulation of text. In our view, Roberts' proposals (1962) substantially misinterpret Chomsky's theory and intentions. One is never sorry, of course, to find teachers making useful and intelligent simplification of complicated linguistic systems to further their teaching of language, but the confusion of text with grammatical rules, if it is useful, is so theoretically misleading as to invalidate the claim that it interprets Chomsky.

Roberts' *English Syntax* (1964), is not an application of TG; it is an exposition of part of the grammar. He uses the linear Skinnerian programme — which most teachers will remember is a form of text designed for auto-instruction by proceeding step by step in information (frame by frame) with a question-and-answer test element built into each frame to regulate progress. Roberts recommends his text for college students, but suggests that his book might be used with upper school classes as a grammar book. He hints that writing will improve under its influence, but in fact makes no bold claims for applications. Further, his notion that a school teacher might go through the programme frame by frame with the class not only defeats the purpose of the linear programme form, but clearly shows the course to be concerned more with the exposition of theory than with applications of the grammar to schoolwork.

Roberts' *English Series* (1966–67) is a most extensive school course designed to produce a comprehensive language and literature programme for grades 3–9 inclusive in the American school (ages 10–17). TG is used as the device for explaining sentence structure in the writing course. The lessons are very tightly scheduled and a teacher's book instructs the class teacher in very great detail how to conduct each lesson, how to answer pupils' questions, how to interpret literary texts studied, etc. This course has been held to be 'teacher-proof' and this aspect of the series, together with its authoritarian use of linguistic theory has led to unrest among certain educationists and linguists, culminating in an outspoken attack by Wayne O'Neil (1968) in which he alleges that Roberts misuses linguistic theory and distorts applications at the expense of well-established classroom practice; that he endangers school reform by these distortions; that he misuses terms from theory, such as 'elegance' and 'simplicity', using them as kudos terms and leaving them open to lay interpretation, thus deluding the public. O'Neil points out that spoken English is subordinated to written English in Roberts' course. Further, Roberts manipulates the English of his course to make it fit his linguistic theory, for example by using a simplified form of literary written English as his teaching model to make it fit Chomsky's phrase-structure rules. (See also Chapter 4 on this point.)

Clearly, this is a most vicious attack, and one, in the face of it, almost rushes to support Roberts against it. But O'Neil makes good sense in much of it, even if he seems intemperate in some of his remarks. O'Neil and other commentators remind us that we are faced with a serious controversy about the wisdom and reliability of applications of TG.

Since this is an area of debate in which teachers can expect some involvement in the next few years, some remarks about the grammar itself and the special difficulties of its applications may be helpful. In the first place, Chomsky's view of the role of linguistics is anti-empiricist. His concern is not with empirically verified description of observed utterances, but with rationally vindicated properties of systems of rules which account for human language (1966a:10). There is some value in recalling that in the 1957 treatise, Chomsky proposed TG as an evaluating device for existing grammars, and not as a description of a given language. This evaluation is carried out in the most abstract and rationalistic dimension; it characterises the speaker's ability to produce language rather than accounts for observed utterances. Chomsky is, as he claims in a recent lecture (1968b) both psychologist and linguist.

One of the most important of Chomsky's theoretical proposals is that we should distinguish in our linguistics questions of *competence* from those of *performance*. Competence is tacit conceptual knowledge — what Chomsky defined in *Aspects* (1965:4) as 'the speaker-hearer's knowledge of his language'. Performance refers to the actual use of language — including the idiosyncracies of a given speaker, the *um*'s and *ah*'s, the slips of the tongue, the memory lapses and the like. Performance would only resemble competence if the speaker were an ideal speaker and his hearers were ideal hearers. But competence underlies all performance, and, in a strangely circular way, depends on it, since statements about competence are ultimately verified by being part of performance. The idea of underlying competence in TG theory is one of highly abstract characterisation of the rules of grammar. Chomsky has asserted several times (1965, etc.) that it is highly unlikely that a study of the actual output of language by a speaker would reveal anything significant about the nature of the language in use. What lies behind language performance, he argues, is, not surprisingly, a very complicated device by which the mind allocates linguistic structure to the language noises we hear. Since every heard utterance is new to the hearer, and since each uttered sentence is new to the speaker (i.e. is *created*) the abstract ability of the speaker to encode and decode is the vital aspect of language which we must characterise.

A teacher, therefore, should think of TG theory as not being concerned with utterances, but with the theoretical identity of sentences. In terms of language production, Chomsky is concerned with those aspects of mind which concern themselves with language (1968b). His interest is therefore in linguistics as an aspect of philosophy or psychology, and his standpoint in this sphere of scholarship is that of a rationalist. He is concerned with what have been called necessary aspects of language production, as opposed to the contingencies of actual language in use. In effect this puts his ideas out of reach of ordinary classroom application, unless it be that the ideas – the philosophy – of TG act as informing notions, helping the teacher to understand better the problem of language as a problem of mind (one almost wants to spell it the Problem of Language).

Robert Lees, defending Chomsky's position at a conference, said in 1964 that if you ask a structuralist question, you get a structuralist answer, and his point is well made. Theories by their nature determine the sort of information they can retrieve. But if this is true of structuralism, it is also true of TG. If you ask a rationalist theoretician a question about the competence of a speaker, it will be treated as a question within philosophy and not directly related to the linguistic exploration and comprehension of texts, or the composition of sentences in any classroom sense, or utterances we have heard on a bus. Chomsky's proposals have undoubted value for teachers, but not as a kind of text analysis, likely to produce a methodology for the classroom.

The term 'generative' in Chomsky's theory is critical to the proper understanding of TG. It is not used in its lay sense of 'produce'. Unfortunately, this term, and several others in TG like 'competence', 'elegance', 'transformation', have become widely misinterpreted by teachers, as McNeill (1968) notes. The notion of creative use of language in speech and writing which has directed much of the latest work in English has made some teachers link Chomsky's prestigious remarks about the creation of language with creative writing or creative talk in the classroom. *Generative* means two things in TG theory: (i) that the theory is maximally predictive and (ii) that it is maximally formal in its proofs. (Lyons, 1968:155.) Roberts (1967) in the teachers' section of his *Series*, just after dismissing the generative approach to grammar as something he has no time to explain to teachers at that point, clearly implies that 'generate' means 'produce'. Markwardt, in a disappointingly short and misleading passage (1966:24) deals with the confusion in teachers' minds between 'transformational' and 'generative' thus: 'The term *generative* applies to the aim of grammatical study . . . which is here presumed to be productive rather than analytical'. He showed that he believed that generative grammar was the latest form of description (1966:25) and that it 'comes to grips with syntax directly'. Markwardt was either unaware of Thomas's excellent book *Transformational Grammar and the Teacher of English* (1965) or he opted to ignore it, because Thomas explicitly discusses the fault of equating *generate* and *produce* (1965:8). O'Neil, in the attack on Roberts we have already referred to above accuses Markwardt of promoting myopia and 'totally misinforming the educational world about the crucial issues in linguistics and related disciplines' (1968:14).

Clearly, the coming of TG has not in any way lessened the debate between teacher and linguist, and in some ways it has produced a polemic which is as violent as Bloomfield's was in the early stages of structuralism. The debate about TG is by no means restricted to applications of linguistics in education. Psychologists and philosophers are deeply concerned by some of Chomsky's assertions about their fields. While there have been fertile developments in psycholinguistics because of Chomsky since his mathematical approach is ideally suited to computation and in philosophy since Chomsky is part logician in his theory, there have also been some brickbats thrown. For instance, Esper, in a book examining the relationship between psychology, philosophy and linguistics (essentially the linguistics stemming from Bloomfield's work) claims that Chomsky, by becoming a latter day Cartesian, has revived antique views of language and other moribund doctrines, mentalism, nativism (the *faculté de langage* approach to child language acquisition), intuitionism and cognitive theories of psychology (1968). Some psychologists would like to 'shoo' Chomsky off their patch; some philosophers feel that Chomsky is reviving issues laid to rest by philosophy in the eighteenth century.

There is at least one sense in which the notion of transformation in TG finds acceptance by teachers of language. The definition of transformation in its weakest form might be held to refer to any process by which hypothesised underlying structure might be related to the actual output of language in utterance. In its strong form, the definition of transformation is of T-rules which operate on the symbols of deep structure and relate them to the symbols of output. Leaving aside the 'calculus' definition, which TG theoreticians would insist on, there is a way of relating the notion of transformation in its weak definition to language teaching practice, without crudely stating it as conversion rules as Roberts (1962) did. Lyons has tentatively suggested that the idea of conversion which lay behind the well-known rules for the writing of *oratio obliqua* from a given sentence of *oratio recta* in Latin might be said to be an imprecise formulation of trans-form rules (1968:174,253). But this interesting and possible interpretation of the term 'transformation' – the weak inter-pretation referred to above – would not be acceptable to Chom-sky. He rejects the temptation to give an organised account of 'many useful procedures in analysis' because he doubts whether these could be formulated rigorously, exhaustively and simply enough to qualify as a practical aid to discovery procedures. (1957:56). In this we should note Chomsky's extreme caution in making claims for his grammar, particularly in his publications between 1957 and 1965. For instance, he denies that it is practical (as we noted), that it is intuitive, and that it can be justified by introspection (1957:56). In *Syntactic Structures* (1957) and *Aspects* (1965) and particularly clearly in *Topics* (1966) he argues that school approaches should be devised by educationists, with particular focus on their educational goals. Most teachers would be happy to agree with Chomsky in this; the requirements of teaching are quite distinct from those of formulisation and vindication of the theory.

There is direct evidence that Chomsky himself does not want applications of TG in teaching at present. He has argued powerfully, in his review (1959) of Skinner's *Verbal Behavior* (1957) that the psychology underlying much of recent educa-tional theory is defective. Further, in 1966, addressing teachers of foreign languages, he asserted that neither linguistics nor psychology was in a state fit for applications at that time. In more recent years, 1968 and 1969 for example, Chomsky has taken up a more open stand as a philosopher and psychologist. His *Language and Mind* asserts that linguistics is merely an aspect of psychology (1968b). This has been further elaborated in a BBC radio talk (1968a) and in his John Locke Lectures, given in Oxford in 1969. He seems to have said very little about the formulation of TG in these recent years and to have focused more on what might loosely be called the social implications of language theory. This change of emphasis is closely connected with difficulties within TG relating to the handling of semantics. Much of this is of peripheral interest only to teachers, but for those interested in the progress of ideas the latest Chomsky titles are fascinating reading – and are much more readable than his early works, which were jargon bound. Finally, Lyons' splendid little book *Chomsky* (1970) presents a very clear and exciting picture of the man and his theories which any well-informed teacher of language or languages should read at the first opportunity.

# 4 The Nature of a Teaching Grammar

Education is one of the principal consumers of grammar. To be precise, one should say that education is a consumer of grammars, since there is ample evidence of different theories of grammar being effectively adapted for teaching purposes. More seriously, there is also ample evidence of education over-enthusiastically embracing a given grammatical theory and applying it in a short-sighted and doctrinaire way to its teaching programmes, making in the process claims for its value with something like evangelical fervour. Nevertheless, it is very clear to any teacher who reads widely in applied linguistics that there is considerable value both for the teacher and for the syllabus in considering on the positive side the nature and value of a pedagogical grammar, and on the negative side in reminding ourselves of the cardinal sins of brash application of linguistic theory to educational practice.

The teacher of language finds himself in a very demanding position in considering which grammar he should apply. He is, clearly if uneasily, placed between the identified needs of the learners and the difficult and often bewildering world of academic linguistics. What most educationists recognise clearly is that academic linguistics is a vigorous and exciting field of intellectual enquiry. Perhaps no area of humanistic enquiry in recent years has commanded so much interest and, equally, has raised so many fertile issues about human language and thought. Theoretical linguistics, with its aim of throwing light on the nature of human language seems to have applications to questions of learning, because language is learned; to social questions, since language is a vital element in society; to philosophy, since so many problems resolve themselves as problems of expression and formulation. With strong inter-disciplinary links like these, it is not surprising to find appliers violently disagreeing over the kind of grammars needed for various consumers, and over the interpretation of these grammars in the hands of the consumers.

If disagreement were limited to the consumers, all might still be well, but the vigorous world of linguistic theory is itself locked in debate on the merits of different theories and on the aims of linguistic approaches. The teacher is thus, as a potential consumer, asked to make clear judgements about his needs as an applier of grammars; but he is also asked to judge what aspects of linguistic theory might be of use to him in his teaching. The latter judgement is one of extraordinary difficulty. A teacher is in fact asked to be an eclectic in linguistic theory, selecting what he thinks might be useful for his needs. But being an eclectic implies knowing the field, and in practice very few teachers know enough about linguistics to judge clearly what is available. Inevitably the vast intelligence of a given theory, or the prestige or persuasiveness of academics, or the mere availability of certain more fully documented theories than others may make teachers choose partially. The really important issue for educational applications of grammar (and other aspects of linguistics) is that the teacher should first identify his teaching needs and should critically examine available linguistic theory afterwards in the light of his diagnosis. This order of events is the only healthy one. A teacher who reels tipsily back to his classroom after drinking deeply of linguistic theory and who fuzzily applies what he thinks the theory states, regardless of educational needs, is a danger to the whole notion of intelligent co-operation between linguistic theory and educational practice.

The problems of efficient application of grammars are probably more obvious in second or foreign language teaching than in work in the mother-tongue. For example, many teachers of immigrants in Britain have had to think seriously about whether a teaching grammar which would link Jamaican Creole and English could be devised. A teacher knowing areas of fruitful analogy and areas of interference between the mother-tongue and English might be able to operate more effectively. Thomas (1965:5) has suggested that a grammar for native speakers is inevitably different from one designed to teach foreign learners;[1] further, each foreign language family would require a different pedagogical grammar. This view, which is based on studies in contrastive linguistics has adherents in applied linguistics, but it also has numerous opponents. Nida (1960) mentions it as a sin of application that a teaching grammar should foist on the mother-tongue features of language present only in the foreign language to be learned. For example the notion of passive, middle and active voices in Greek can be illustrated in English although it does not contribute to an accurate description of English, even if the knowledge of 'middleness' can be shown to help the learning of Greek voice.[2]

Progressive education has always distinguished itself by its ability to apply theory in non-doctrinaire ways to pragmatic ends, and it has been the experience of most teacher-appliers of linguistics that theorists look sympathetically on this kind of eclecticism. They may point out that it ceases to be pure linguistics, but they respect the priorities involved for education. We repeat, the most distressing form of educational application of linguistic grammars is found where teachers expound a linguistic theory as a new-found body of knowledge which, willy nilly, pupils must learn. Thus the new-found grammar becomes an explicit part of education, not a teaching aid. It is this kind of application, where linguistics creates a new subject in the school syllabus, that leads to acrimony among teachers and between educationist and academic.

For instance, questions of the form of a phrase-structure grammar, the sort of issue debated hotly by Postal (1964), is an issue for linguistics, but how to analyse a sentence or clause or phrase for teaching purposes is purely a question for education.[3] Yet Roberts applies a simple phrase-structure grammar in his *English Series*, virtually proposing linguistics as a content subject for American primary and secondary schools. His applications are seen by O'Neil of Harvard (1968) as '. . . no more than jokes, a veneer of linguistics, a few arrows and other symbols from the grammarian's bag of tricks' : O'Neil, like many educationists, would resist *any* calculus of rules of class materials. Reading Roberts closely, some teachers, one suspects, would resent even more the authoritarian tone of presentation, certain to frighten the timid and persuade the weak. A really alarming aspect of the *Series* is that it is openly held to be 'teacher proof'. It makes provision in elaborate teacher notes for almost every question likely to arise in classwork and for literature and linguistics and indeed, for everything likely to arise, a clear-cut answer is given. This so misrepresents the relationship which should exist between a teacher, his pupils and a textbook, that few teachers in Britain at least could use the series in any strict way. Roberts obviously had a different standpoint in methodology from many of us, and lest many should think that his method is the consequence of his interest in linguistics, and should condemn one with the other, we would point out that any maximally expository course (like a simple linear programme in any subject) may take on the appearance of being teacher-proof.[4] Yet it is indisputable that one of the effects of the *Series* has been that many liberal educationists have been shocked by Roberts' methodological approach into rejecting 'linguistics' as a course shaping device.

We would do well to distinguish questions of method from questions of linguistic theory underlying a course. Some scholars have seen this as a distinction of procedure as opposed to theory (Allen, 1957:16). Allen pleads that applications of linguistic theory in school texts should be left to 'individual craftsmen'. A teacher would thus, in expounding a text, or leading his class through a piece of argument, a poem, or indeed any piece of language, ancient or modern, resort to linguistic theory as an instrument of description or explanation. One has often called this 'getting a handhold on the experience of language'. Linguistic theory, in this approach, is taken to be available to the teacher in some quantity and in some richness. Allen puts the case well for the incidental application of linguistics. One might see this as an argument parallel to those advanced for the incidental use of economic theory in modern studies, for sociology in history and for advanced mathematical theory in modern 'experimental' mathematics in the schools.

This is the weakest case for the applications of linguistics in schoolwork and it has a great deal to recommend it. To achieve an unobtrusive and effective incidental application of linguistics of this order, however, requires a teaching staff widely and thoroughly trained in linguistics. This is the paradox; either our teachers of English must be able to judge independently on a good linguistic basis, or we run the risk of over-application and misapplication of the theory. The more linguistic (and methodological) training, the less likely we will be to find over-enthusiastic misapplications; the less thoroughly our people are trained, the higher the likelihood of evangelical fervour, half-truths and dogmatic content teaching of linguistics.

The strong case for school applications of linguistics has presented linguistics as 'new grammar'. Although this view was assisted by the presence of the keenly apologetic linguistics of Bloomfield, it was not entirely produced by pressure from academics. It was aided and abetted by a mechanistic view of learning based on simple stimulus-response learning theory; it was aggrandised by notions of being a technology in an age of vast technological advance; in methodology it coincided with an American revival of interest in learning as instruction. The effects on teachers of this coincidence of pressures was sometimes one of bewilderment. Quite often teachers would ask linguists what the new grammar in fact was – was there a simple book on it? etc. Teachers were led to believe that traditional grammar, and all it stood for in schoolwork, was discredited. While this 'new grammar' movement was most pronounced in America in the fifties, British education did not escape entirely, although few doctrinaire structuralist textbooks were in fact used in schools here. British teachers have been independent of the prescribed grammar book for too long to be easily won back.

Teachers can hardly be blamed for yielding to the great pressures from above in this 'new grammar' movement. Prominent academics loudly proclaimed that a 'revolution' had taken place (Francis, 1954; Levin, 1960). Many articles appeared in American teaching journals advocating immediate change over to structural grammar. Pooley (1957) for example, lists fourteen articles in the *English Journal* alone between January 1953 and November 1956. Fries (1954) made a memorable, jaunty attack on the definition of the sentence and on traditional grammar in general. In journals and at numerous conferences, both in America and, later, in Britain, there was a tendency for the message to reduce itself to a slogan 'Old grammar bad; new grammar good'.

We should perhaps note that Pooley (1957) was a more cautious advocate of the new grammar than many of his contemporaries. He suggested that all the activity among teachers which had led to the fourteen articles he cited, argued that teachers wanted a new grammar. He went on to suggest that a new grammar was available in structural linguistics. His suggestions for a teaching grammar are, in fact, often quite reasonable, combining a structural view of text with a not untraditional view of meaning. But Pooley, we believe, mistook the nature of the protest. Teachers who write advocating a change over to structural grammars may merely be stating in an extreme form an aversion to the methods and practices of traditional 'instructional' courses in old grammar. Secondly, Pooley to some extent misled his public by suggesting that there was a shining, new, fully-fledged grammar available. Gleason (1964) makes the very valid point that for some decades there has been considerable activity in the writing of parts of grammars – tracts on grammar we might call them – but that no substantial grammar of English on the scale of Sweet or Jespersen had emerged.[6] What was new in the new grammar was attitude, and this was valuable. What was misleading, and finally demoralising for some teachers, was that a transitory approach within a broad development of linguistic theory was mistaken for a new and permanent philosophy

65

of grammar which would solve all the accumulated problems of the school syllabus.

A pedagogic grammar for mother-tongue speakers, whether implicit or explicit in a course, is principally concerned with giving pupils the opportunity to come to grips with aspects of their own *organising* ability in using language, or the organising ability shown by authors or speakers in the texts studied. The goal of a grammar of this sort is therefore to produce a rational, manipulable and communicable metalanguage for the description of utterances studied. It is at this point that we become aware that there is a basic incompatibility between educational requirements and linguistic theory. A linguistically explicit theory is distinguished by its rationale. It should produce a 'watertight' structural analysis of the phenomena of language if it is 'descriptive' and it should produce an incontrovertible explanation of the organisation of language if it is 'generative'.

Requirements of theory are particular to the theoretical approach; at best they may all be related to the philosophy of science or to a particular form of logic, but they may have little more in common. Theory is consistent when it is internally consistent and can be shown to explain within its own prescriptions recognisable phenomena of the data. Wars between theorists are usually over validation of a theory and over its explanatory power. We should not forget that linguistics is a world of many theories opposed on details and frequently on fundamentals. Questions asked by education may be incomprehensible to linguists, partly because the logic of a given linguistic theory may be vastly different from the logic of an educational question, but also because linguistic theoreticians may have a defective, or non-existent knowledge of education. Just as a teacher may seem like a layman to a linguistic theoretician, so a theoretical linguist may seem crude in his views on education when he attempts to legislate for the teacher.

We can illustrate the difficulty teachers might find in asking questions about language by referring to an interesting discussion which arose in the mid-sixties on the nature of linguistic enquiry. Lees and Bolinger, two prominent linguists, argued the respective cases of the generative or 'model-centred' and the descriptive or 'data-centred' points of view.[5] They used the analogy of the entomologist. Under a structuralist interpretation (i.e. descriptive) an entomologist is a collector of bugs. He may devise ways of arranging his collection and classifying what he has found in nature, but essentially he is restricted to what he finds and how

66

he classifies it. From the generative point of view an entomologist is concerned with the 'bughood' of bugs. Translated back into linguistic theory this means that descriptive theories are concerned with classification of corpuses of heard or read language; generative theories are concerned with the sentencehood of sentences. In a broader framework, descriptive theories are positivist; generative theories are rationalist.

Issues like this show that there is a basic incompatibility between linguistic theory and educational practice since there are issues within linguistics which would make a teacher's questions about language seem irrelevant to the burning issues of theory. But although there is incompatibility, there is not necessarily divorce. We have already stressed the idea of selection from linguistic theory for various teaching needs. Further, a properly trained specialist teacher of English should be aware of the field of theory to the extent that he knows whom to direct his questions to and what sort of things he might profitably ask. The important thing for teachers is that they should be able to judge what they need from linguistics, since they are the consumers; if there are or have been fatuous questions and gross misapplications of theory in the past, it is a reflection on the quality of teacher training, in part at least.

In brief, the effective role played by linguistics in the formation of a pedagogic grammar, or in shaping a course informed by such a grammar, is that of guidance. Linguistic theory can stimulate a teacher, orientate him to his problems, help to rationalise the steps he takes in grading of materials, and assist in the evaluation of progress in the mother-tongue syllabus. Where description obtrudes in teaching, linguistics can usefully guide the form of the metalanguage the teacher may use (or can provide the teacher with a selection of approaches to the *describendum*). Finally, as we shall discuss in subsequent chapters, linguistics has played a very important part in the research which lies on the margins of teaching — child language acquisition and issues of later language learning, which in turn act as orientating forces to the benefit of education.

## NOTES

[1] Thomas, O. (1965) *Transformational Grammar and the Teacher of English*, see p. 5. Thomas's Introductory passages should be prescribed reading for all teachers. He characterises TG swiftly and limits its application in certain sectors of education.

[2] Verbs like μεταφέρομαι 'I am being transported' are passive in both English

and Greek; verbs like κοιμοῦμαι 'I sleep' λυποῦμαι 'I am sorry' are active in English, but are passive in Greek. If we identify these 'middle verbs' in an informal semantic class defined as denoting states of being or feeling, we can introduce a middle voice into English for pedagogic purposes.

[3] Postal, P. (1964) *Constituent Structure* is a synopsis and critique of grammars that appear to him to be phrase-structure grammars. Phrase-structure grammars are closely related to grammars in which the *immediate constituents* of a unit of language are identified and further analysed into their smaller underlying elements, e.g. sentence becomes Noun Phrase (Subject) and Verb Phrase (Predicate); NP becomes adjective + noun, etc. etc. Phrase-structure grammars concern themselves with the *rules* for split•ing language units thus. Whether Postal is right in assuming that some of the grammars he criticises *are* phrase-structure grammars is a most interesting point.

[4] Roberts, P. (1966) *The Roberts English Series* illustrates this well. He prints class question and answer, briefs the teacher extensively and in his text scripts the teacher–pupil encounter. It was this attempt to be 'teacher-proof' that led to Wayne O'Neil's explosion in 1968 (see bibliography).

[5] Broadly, data-centred linguistics began from a corpus of observed text – say a tape of recorded speech – while model-centred linguistics concentrates on characterising some form of 'device' or mathematical (or other) model which characterises the competence of the speaker. Model-centred linguistics is a theorist's conception and is concerned with the properties of the theory itself. It does not purport to describe texts.

[6] Since writing this sentence, the long-awaited, comprehensive Grammar of Contemporary English of Quirk, Greenbaum, Leech and Svartvik has emerged. This is the most significant grammar of English this century.

# 5 The Native Speaker and Initial Language Learning

There are many statements and inferences in the literature of education to the effect that teachers of the mother-tongue (and, some would argue, of second or foreign languages) should go back to acquisition studies for orientation to language learning problems in general. The list of distinguished scholars who have made this point is impressive. Carroll (1960) in one of his highly competent summaries of psycholinguistic research, points to the orientation curriculum studies have received from language acquisition research. Mackey (1965) writing from the point of view of analysing the fields of language study relevant to language teaching argues that no analysis of teaching method of first or second languages can be complete without an insight to initial acquisition.[1] Naturally, in the study of abnormal development in language, acquisition studies are counted as vitally important for diagnosis, and by corollary, for establishing norms of language learning and language use. In some recent work, acquisition studies are used as part of the discussion of 'readiness' in learning. Perhaps most significant of all in connection with our present discussion is the strong common sense urge one meets among teachers to believe that how we first acquired our native language has more than academic interest for the later handling of language teaching in school.[2]

Psychologists also display a high and continuing interest in linguistic studies of language acquisition. Teachers interested in this might like to refer to that interesting collection of papers edited by Smith and Miller (1966) to find some of the best minds in psychology involved with many of the latest ideas in linguistics in a quest to discover more about the acquisition of language in the child. While there is a case for arguing that many psychologists have been just too quick in applying linguistic theory to language research of this kind, sometimes finding themselves applying linguistic theory which has been jettisoned by the theorists shortly after being advanced, it is true to say that the sixties saw theories of language and theories of mind rapidly and significantly coming together. At times theories of language and mind undoubtedly make uneasy bedfellows, but most of us are intuitively aware that linguistics and psychology have been the poorer by being separated in recent decades. The main drift of Chomsky's theories of language in recent years has been towards the linguist giving more than a rationalisation of language; he is now also concerned with the theory of mind.

Teachers who follow through the literature will find widely different theoretical positions adopted by the research listed. One finds traditional grammar and structural grammar used, with numerous phonetic systems for dealing with the sounds the child makes. There are innumerable personal variations on recognisable linguistic themes. Since the early sixties, however, the effect of Chomsky on acquisition studies has been clearly marked. His emphasis on the 'creative' side of human organisation of speech and his interest in the universals of linguistic theory have set him up in direct opposition to the more mechanistic approaches which we loosely refer to as 'behaviouristic' studies of acquisition, which deal largely with notions of stimulus, response and reinforcement derived from Skinner and which often link their experimental procedures with Bloomfield's structuralist linguistics.

The most recent work in child language acquisition shows two main features. Firstly, there is an open unwillingness to accept 'data-reduction' techniques of dealing with language, and the simplistic bracketing procedures which often accompany data-reduction on the linguistic side.[3] Secondly, there is a rejection of stimulus-response learning as a plausible model of psycholinguistic interest. Consider the data problem involved. A researcher who has tapes of child language noises cannot assume that, by merely listening to them and listing the categories of sound or utterance he thinks he can hear, he has, in any relevant way, described the process of acquisition. To begin with the researcher's linguistic theory may foist on to the sounds on the tape classifications and categories which are likely to be misleading — like trying to establish whether the child uses adverbs before adjectives in an acquisition sequence, or whether the child uses the past tense of strong verbs before weak ones. Also, in terms of stimulus and response learning theory we have a remarkable argument put forward very commonly — that the child imitates what it hears and retains what is reinforced by the parents or others. But what we know of casual colloquial speech leads us to believe that it is highly defective as a basis for the production of the sentences of a language (Chomsky's point); further, parents have the habit of reinforcing the coy, the unusual and the cute words used by a baby. In many cases the parents reinforce what would be irrelevant for the correct acquisition of the tongue. Their own 'baby talk' often forms a most curious corpus of speech. While we are not arguing that babies should be addressed in Macaulayesque English, we would insist that S–R theories, so insistent on imitation, are based on a set of peculiar premises as far as language acquisition is concerned.

In acquisition studies, as in linguistic theory in general, Chomsky's 'great innovation', as Thorne has called it (1965), is the shifting of the emphasis in our thinking about language from the organisation of what we hear (or the *apparent* organisation of that data) to explanation of that organisation. Our studies now centre on the organising power of the human speaker which is capable of producing the sentences of a language. What we manage to collect on tape or in our notebooks is a trivial portion only of the language and what we might say after bracketing our collection of sentences in one way or another would be at best a very weak explanation of the power of language.

If we think a little more about the 'creative' theory of acquisition suggested by work done by Chomsky, we find many ideas of interest to teachers of language, but we also detect certain peculiarities of the logic of the approach. Firstly, we must never forget that Chomsky's work is in language theory and not in any particular application of that theory. Thus Chomsky is often polemical in what he writes, for instance in his trenchant dismissal of Skinner's stimulus-response model of verbal behaviour (1959). He has claimed consistently for a decade 'There are no known principles of association or reinforcement and no known sense of 'generalisation' that can begin to account for this characteristic 'creative' aspect of language learning and use' (1968).

It is well known that TG grammarians propose a Language Acquisition Device (LAD) as part of their rationalisation of the creation of language. This is the 'black-box' theory. Into this LAD what Chomsky calls 'primary linguistic data' is fed, and by means yet unknown, the child produces a grammar of the language. Elizabeth Ingram, in a review of recent studies of language acquisition (1969) put this point: 'The LAD is merely a black box inside which all the interesting things happen. . . . It is not an explanation, merely a disguise for the lack of one.'

The grammar produced by the LAD contains what Chomsky calls a set of language universals, 'which are not learned ; rather they provide the organising principles that make language

71

learning possible. (Such categories) must exist if data is to lead to knowledge' (1966). His notion of creativeness in language learning thus stands on a three-fold argument. Firstly, that language universals set a limit to the kind of language a child will learn. Secondly, language universals are necessary for language learning. Thirdly, language is 'creative' because it draws on a set of innate ideas which interpret the raw data of language and allow the learner actually to learn the language of his community. A child, then, learns his own native tongue by doing what later learners might also be said to do – he constructs for himself an internalised grammar which acts as a heuristic ('discovery') device, that is a device for interpreting, structuring and retaining language.

It should not escape our attention that the 'creative' argument advanced by Chomsky postulates linguistic universals as a theoretically necessary part of the LAD. Then, by a drift of dialectic, Chomsky first juxtaposes then equates linguistic universals and innate ideas. His whole position on this is rationalist, in the manner of Descartes and the rationalist philosophers of the seventeenth century. He bases much of his recent work in this area on Humboldt. Readers who are interested in this aspect of Chomsky's thought should read that brief but most readable of his books, *Language and Mind* (1968b) in the first chapter of which he makes his position very clear; a more detailed philosophical statement is made in *Cartesian Linguistics* (1966b).

It is not always easy for the layman to follow Chomsky and his disciples, not only because their ideas are difficult, but because their publications are couched in a jargon and a symbolism which daunt all but the most determined readers. Happily, several good analyses of Chomsky's position *vis-à-vis* child language acquisition are available. Mrs. Ingram's excellent review *Recent Trends in Psycholinguistics: A Critical Notice* (1969) presents a splendid analysis of Chomsky's position and raises numerous issues about the suitability of using TG theory for child language study.

She points out, for instance, that there has been some retraction on the question of specifying the language universals in the acquisition process. McNeill, early in 1966 (1966a) postulated as universals the phrase structure part (the P-rules) of the grammar and a system of item classification in sentences, – 'pivot' and 'open' (*that's X; that's Y*, etc., where *that's* is the pivot). Later in 1966 (1966b) after studying a Japanese child

72

in some detail, McNeill withdrew the 'hierarchical classificatory system' of pivot and open classes and left only the phrase structure as a universal. In effect McNeill seemed to suggest that two children, closely studied, would yield two sets of linguistic universals. And three children? *Ad infinitum?*

If we are to use acquisition studies as a source of enlightenment in our consideration of mother-tongue language work in later school years, we have at least several important issues to face. Linguistic universals exist as a concept within linguistic theory, and, despite what Chomsky is now saying about the continuity between theories of language and theories of mind (*Cartesian Linguistics* (1966b); *Language and Mind* (1968b), etc.) it is worth remembering that it is not usual to regard a statement about grammar as a statement about learning, and that many of the gravest pedagogical mistakes in the past have arisen from this point. Chomsky may well have provided us with a fruitful concept in his arguments for a 'creative' aspect of language learning, and indeed of all language use, however. A child in a very real sense does create for himself a grammar from defective examples of the spoken language of his early environment. In some useful sense when a human being speaks he utters sentences *de novo*.[4] Further, Chomsky argues (as an afterthought to his chapter on Language Acquisition in *Cartesian Linguistics*, 1966) that 'cognitive power' is properly called *mind* only if it is in some sense 'creative' (a point originally made by Descartes). This idea and others that we have discussed above, present us with a useful, imaginative, if highly abstract basis from which to rationalise our problems of mother-tongue acquisition and teaching. But we would do well to recall that, at this stage in our knowledge of both linguistics and psychology, we accept these proposals as an elaborate metaphor, rather than in any sense proof positive of the nature of language or the human mind.

One of the problems which arise in teachers' minds on the interpretation of Chomsky may be stated thus: if we hold that a human child has a *faculté de langage*, and if we mean by this merely that language is human-specific (therefore is *not* learned by animals) then we are making a very weak claim for our linguistics-and-learning theory. If we uphold the strong claim, however, we may find ourselves jockeyed into the position where we must hold (as Colin Fraser pointed out) that the child is now born with *Aspects of the Theory of Syntax* (1965 version!) tucked away inside.

Most of us would agree with Fraser (Lyons and Wales, 1966) that it is a good guess that the child has innate language acquiring power; that it is a good guess that the nature of this innate language-acquiring power takes the form of a control of the fundamentals of his own language, which by argument *may* be shown to be linguistic universals; but not all of us would want to accept that the nature of the internalised universals was identical with the current or most fashionable linguistic notions in academic theory. One detects considerable concern in Lyons' remark; 'I have no views on the plausibility of the *faculté de langage* as a psychological hypothesis; but I am a little disturbed by the readiness with which some psychologists have interpreted Chomsky's arguments (1965) about the formal and substantive "universals" of syntactic theory as evidence in support of this'. (Lyons and Wales, 1966.)

It would be a perfectly healthy and fertile point of view for a teacher to hold that all learning, including language learning in and of the mother-tongue, was based on 'interpretative principles' or innate ideas (call them what you will). This is a notion of long standing and of considerable intellectual importance. The idea of there being some underlying fundamental rationalising or 'interpretative' principles would seem to be Cartesian, and probably originally Platonic. Lord Herbert of Cherbury, for instance (1624), is quoted by Chomsky on this issue of thought. 'Without them (i.e. interpretative principles of thought) we could have no experiences at all, or be capable of observation . . . If we had not been endowed with common notions . . . we should never come to distinguish between things or grasp any general nature . . . We possess hidden faculties, which, when stimulated by objects, quickly respond to them' (Chomsky, 1966:105–6). It would seem perfectly plausible to read 'language' for 'objects' in this remark and to take Herbert's statement as a language acquisition model. The general notion of interpretative principles, however, is much more acceptable than the highly formulated idea of the phrase-structure grammar being present as an interpretative principle, as McNeill urges (1966a, b).

Equating linguistic ideas with learning processes is a step which, we believe, most teachers would be unwilling to take, although they might find themselves inclining towards the idea of the human speaker having some kind of *faculté de langage* which makes it possible for him to learn language at all. Yet researchers into child language often find it necessary to assume

74

that linguistics and learning equate. This state of affairs has been produced partly by the wide currency Chomsky's ideas have in both linguistics and psychology; further, Chomsky's ideas are mathematico-logical in form and lend themselves to certain experimental treatment. To argue thus, however, is a typical case of the tail wagging the dog. If linguistic description or explanation is an instrument of enquiry, it ought to be subordinate to the general philosophy of the enquiry – be a servant to it and not a master. Yet the power and prestige of TG is such that in several instances in education and experimentation it has forced the experiment into assumptions which are, to say the least, speculative. Child language study can show numerous instances of this.

An alternative approach to Chomsky's has produced interesting results (1970) in the hands of at least one child language survey team, the Nuffield Project which worked in Edinburgh under Dr. T. Ingram. This team pointed out that what the child intends to communicate is of vital importance. If we try to characterise the semantic relationships of the utterance and its situation we can construct a 'production grammar' of his speech. This work owes much to Fillmore's case grammar proposals.[5] Van Buren, a member of the Edinburgh team, has drawn up a model for handling the description of child utterances. The mother and an observer interpret the situation in which the child meaningfully utters the language and by a semantic characterisation this forms – like Fillmore's underlying case relationships – a deep set of relationships which can be linked to the output of language by a kind of realisation process. It is transformationally related to the output by a series of rules. Teachers will recognise in this a model which has affinity with traditional grammar approaches. Meaning defines loosely the underlying network of relationships, and the formal side of grammar accounts for these relationships appearing in certain ways (perhaps several different ways) at the surface.

We should not be too quick to argue that things have come full cycle, however – traditional–structural–transformational–traditional. What we are in fact witnessing in linguistics is the vindication of a number of long standing scholarly views. Firth's idea that all linguistic description was description of meaning comes to mind. We are witnessing the revival of interest in semantics, and the new interest in the relationships between semantics and grammar. Van Buren's 'production' grammar is a research example of this. Fillmore's 'case grammar' is another.

75

Lyons' 'notional' approach and, in a slightly different dimension, Halliday's 'systemic grammar' all bear this out. All see semantics as an input to grammar, and all formulate in some way the distinction between deep and surface aspects of language. The study of initial language learning has stimulated this movement.

Our consideration in this chapter of some of the problems associated with a satisfactory approach to language learning, and some of the proposals for dealing with these problems cannot bring us to a fixed and proven view of either language or language learning in the child-learner. But as we have argued, the metaphor of 'creative' theories of language acquisition and learning is a fruitful one, and links with some findings of cognitive psychology in subsequent learning, as we shall show in a later chapter. Our suggestion then is this: Native speakers seem to show at the initial stage of language learning that they have underlying faculties which make learning possible. This also makes language learning personal and, in the sense defined above, 'creative'. If initial language learning is to affect what we do in later school work in the sphere of learning and use of the mother-tongue, it is most likely to be in the areas of personal and creative responses to language in use, and in the productive use of language in a form acceptable by the native community.

## NOTES

[1]    The same point appears in Firth (1937), Halliday (1967) and Ingram (1969), and in many other places in the literature of applied linguistics.

[2]    There is a growing realisation among applied linguists that 'the internalisation of a grammar' may characterise both early acquisition of language and the development of later skills (e.g. comprehension) in school use of language. Further, the point, expressed in this book in several places, that all learning is language-bound is a very important dynamic in recent educational discussion. See Halliday (1967d).

[3]    The term 'data-reduction' describes a technique of studying a corpus of say, child language and generalising about it in the light of a theory. Thus a linguist might take a tape of child talk and identify its phonemes, its syntax, its vocabulary, etc.

[4]    There is growing resistance to the idea of every sentence uttered being in some significant linguistic sense novel. Hasan (1968) has put the case forward that the 'creativity' of a sentence is best judged as the way a sentence relates to its context; thus identical forms of sentence might have different contexts. Further, it is difficult as Ingram argues (1969) to accept only one sentence type, which appears to be the position into which we are jockeyed by a generative view of the creativity of utterances.

[5]    Fillmore's case grammar is expounded in his paper *The Case for Case* in Bach and Harms (eds) 1968, Proceedings of the 1967 Texas Conference on

76

Language Universals. Broadly he argues that a generative grammar ought to provide for a series of case relationships in its characterisations. He proposed an informal semantic definition of cases as part of the deep structure of the grammar; this was one of the main lines of enquiry which led to scholars doubting the validity of the TG model proposed by Chomsky in 1965.

# 6 Learning by 'Discovery'

A three-cornered relationship exists between educational method, teaching technique and lesson materials. Of these three, method is the most abstract, defining the theoretical link between the educational aims we have in our teaching and the materials. Usually, method is classified by the way we try to achieve the aim; thus we hear of expository methods, heuristic methods, activity methods and the like. Method is thus the philosophy of our teaching task in a given subject in that it orientates us to the teaching. What we have described as teaching techniques are ways in which this philosophy is realised in actual class lessons. Thus we might use note dictation, silent reading, class discussion or free composition as teaching techniques. Naturally the method we use is likely to be reflected in the technique with which we handle lesson materials, but it is worth remembering that teaching technique is secondary to method in syllabus planning, just as it is in teacher training. First we select aims and methods; then we decide how best to carry them out in an actual teaching situation.

In discussing the nature of initial learning of the mother-tongue we came to the conclusion that certain underlying faculties played a vital part in the learning of language and in the first stages of social use of the native language in Chapter 5. It would be rash to say that we had conclusive knowledge of the nature of these underlying faculties, but the case for the 'creative' view of child language learning, which has been put by Chomsky, and others, indicates that universal ideas of language lie behind the learning. In our view, these are best thought of as underlying semantic notions from which the child organises the deep dependencies and relationships of his language (and probably other aspects of his cognitive life). Thus a teacher dealing with language at later stages in the child's life may make at least a weak link between a 'creative' theory of initial language learning, and the nature of later language learning and use.

The notion of learners constructing learning strategies for themselves based on latent knowledge (or faculties) is well known in the philosophy of education. Leibniz's dictum crystallises it: 'Nothing can be taught us of which we have not already in our minds the idea.' Halliday's view of the underlying resources of language learning puts it as a more social force: a native speaker brings with him an intuitive knowledge of what language is and an awareness of the linguistic structuring of experience (1967d). Thus a socially well adjusted native speaker may be said to have a wide range of intuitions about his own language. He can be held to have these intuitions, or underlying insights, because we see the end product of this 'common sense' about language — that the child is accepted as a native speaker of English in a society speaking English as its native language. On these intuitions the child acts effectively in his whole social and linguistic life; from these latent insights he uses his language as an instrument of other learning. While it may not be proven (if that rather crude term is admissible) that $x$ or $y$ is an underlying faculty or an insight of language learning on which strategies of other learning may rest, it is at least methodologically productive to consider learning from this angle. Further, it is a view which recognises the individuality of the child as well as the basis of his socialisation. It is with this view, that a child already has within his psychological and linguistic make-up the forces we must use for the development of his culture, that we set out our case here.

We can take this 'notion' further. One of the obvious factors limiting slow learners is the low linguistic power of the child. The case is clearest where a language skill, such as reading, is involved, and a child, whose general intellectual progress is initially slow may suddenly accelerate when reading skills improve. Also, Luria and Yudovich (1959) clearly established the relationship between speech development and intellectual ability. At a level deeper than skills, however, a child's ability to encode his responses in acceptable forms indicates his educational and social status, as Bernstein (1965) has suggested. The idea of a 'deprived' linguistic environment is not only related to notions of fluent personal writing, in the terms used by Holbrook (1964) in *English for the Rejected*, but is related to broader educational issues. For example, the child's ability to analyse his situations and reactions, to analogise in the solution of problems (children often display this clearly by talking aloud during psychological manipulation tests), and to devise strategies, is related to encoding power. On an interpretative basis, the ability of the child to rationalise about his environment — on how advertising tries to persuade, or how a joke makes its point etc. — is related both to the ability of the child initially to respond to the advertisement or the joke (etc.) as well as to his power to categorise and discuss the style via his own language. Method must take the linguistic shaping of learning into account.

A crude, but useful distinction exists within educational thought between expository and heuristic approaches in teaching. Expository methods have been caricatured as 'tell-and-do' approaches. Gage (1963) analysed the expository method thus:

1 Stating the item of knowledge to be taught
2 Clarifying the terms of the exposition (e.g. grammatical terms)
3 Justifying the value of the item
4 Reinforcing the exposition by exercises
5 Making transition easy to the next expository stage.

Many English language textbooks, designed for use by native speakers, (and for $L_2$ speakers) make maximum use of the expository method. On the shelves of most English classrooms may be found many old and some new textbooks fashioned rather like this:

RULES OF SYNTAX
Rule1 : The subject of a finite verb must always be in the nominative case; as, *John* comes. / teach.
Observation 1 : The subject may be:

1 A noun; as, *Andrew* is a clever boy.
2 A pronoun; as, *They* are expected today.
3 An adjective with the definite article; as, *The dead* shall arise.
4 An infinitive or infinitive phrase; as, *Teaching attentive boys* is a pleasant occupation.
5 A clause; as, *That he has been rash* is apparent to all.

Then follow exercises of the sort most English teachers will have met: 'Identify the subject in the following sentences'; 'Parse the words in italics'; 'Correct the following sentences'. If the textbooks are old enough some of these may be called 'Promiscuous Exercises'. Textbooks still being used in the fifties in many of our schools had this enthralling heading (indicating, incidentally, a remarkable drift of meaning of the word 'promiscuous').

To argue that this approach is now discredited would be ingenuous. Modern textbooks in common use for public examinations, such as the Higher English examination of the Scottish Certificate of Education, commonly adopt exposition, if not to advocate the approach in school teaching, at least as the most useful form in which the textbook may be cast. For example a textbook published in 1958 for use with these certificate classes dealt with an aspect of subordination of clauses thus:

Types of subordination of the adverbial clause were being taught after the definition of the adverbial clause itself. Notes on some difficult analyses were given (*He was not as clever as his father was. He was not as clever:* principal clause; *as his father was*; subordinate adverbial clause of degree modifying *as clever*). Exceptions and unusual configurations of the adverbial clause were then alluded to and exercises, postponed to the end of the chapter, were given to reinforce the exposition. These exercises were largely parsing and analysis of the sentences of given texts.

It would seem that an expository method would imply in English an axiomatic and fully formalised view of English grammar. Indeed, one often hears teachers speak of traditional formal grammar as if it were in fact a set of axioms. A study of the roots of our school grammars in the nineteenth century, however, reveals anything but a basis of solid axiom. There were several different models to choose from and within the linguistics and rhetoric of the period there were numerous divisions and disagreements both as to method of grammatical analysis and the handling of texts. Perhaps teachers assume, from the expository tone of school grammars such as Nesfield's (1912), that English has inherited a fully worked out mathematical grammar which would support an expository method of Euclidian type rigidity – an axiom is stated; a deduction permitted by logic maps out the consequences; there is empirical confirmation of the rule in a simple operation and, in exercises, further deductions are asked for, or simple productive operations involving applications of the principle are expounded.

If we think loosely of this as the 'scientific' or 'mathematical' method, we very much misrepresent modern school science and mathematics programmes. Statements like this have been common in mathematics guidance for schools since the mid-twenties:

'Geometry is essentially an experimental science like any other, and . . . it should be taught observationally, descriptively and experimentally . . . The child to whom the subject is taught is fundamentally a scientist who lives and learns by experimentation and observation in a wonderful world laboratory.' (Austin, 1927.)

One is tempted to take this statement about 'non-axiomatic, non-expository mathematics' and substitute the words 'English language study' for 'Geometry'. It would substantially characterise some of the objects of this present work and would emphasise the important role of linguistics in language teaching, as the science by which the observer is orientated.

Heuristic methods in teaching are often nicknamed 'discovery methods'. Usually the type of discovery involved in a language teaching heuristic approach is inductive. Basically a heuristic method sets out to make rational the underlying structure of experience. It presents a plan which makes articulate something encountered, e.g. a problem in mathematics, or a feature of language in use. Inductive heuristic methods are characterised by Gage (1963) thus:

1  We present data leading the pupil to hypothesise
2  We present the learner with evidence of the hypotheses acted on
3  We state, or have the learners state, the principle learned inductively from operations 1 and 2.

We could argue that expository and deductive learning stand the cone of learning on its most abstract point. The announced principle – the most abstract aspect of the learning – precedes. The examples and exercises depend on, and assume understanding of, the principle. Thus a child progressing from principle, through examples and exercises presumably reaches the real world of texts and language use after successfully moving from a very abstract piece of learning through diminishing degrees of abstractness to language in real use. If we go further and argue that the most abstract principle of a lesson is the most difficult to grasp, particularly when it precedes all the other work, we see added objections to this approach. Further, if the more intelligent child is the most likely to learn the abstraction (Piaget and Bruner would say also the most mature child), an undue emphasis is placed on intellectual and maturational attainment in the conduct of a general class lesson. Is education only for the intelligent and the mature? Admittedly, exposition can be a rapid method of learning when a very able group of considerable maturity is involved. Thus it is commonly and effectively used in university learning. But does this in itself recommend it to general school use?

Inductive methods begin from native speaking experience in language courses in English. The cone of learning is set safely on its base. The child is first of all brought into contact with a real piece of language in use – a text from the world of written texts known to the child; or an example of speech or writing which the child may himself provide or recognise as a genuine piece of contemporary English in use. From this base the child is led inductively to the principle of description involved. The child reacts to the text or texts presented, either to the function of the text, or an interesting feature of the language text such as how it is expressed, or what it means, or even how it is set out. On this reaction an open class discussion may be based, and in Gage's terms we make the learner aware that he has 'hypothesised'. If the object of the lesson is to add a principle of description to the repertoire of the child – making him more rational and articulate about his own language in use – we can label the inductively realised principle, *if we want to*. We may, on the other hand, feel satisfied with the existence of the child's own recognition of the contrasts involved or the features illustrated in the text, and we may leave the awareness of the feature or features unverbalised. There may in fact be good psychological reason for leaving the principle unverbalised as we shall see later in this chapter when we consider some of the psychological evidence for this approach. But basically this is the inductive approach: reaction to data; discussion of the 'hypothesis'; rationalisation into principles.

Inductive methods in language work begin from native experience, and they cannot be used unless there is a basis from which to work. They derive their main educational dynamic from useful discussion of features recognised or reacted to. In the literature of educational learning some of the most impressive statements about the inductive process have been made: Fisher (1935), discussing the nature of experimentation, declares that 'Inductive inference is the only process . . . by which new knowledge can come into the world'. William James, dealing with the more strictly educational field of learning said that proper learning can only take place when the learner can say 'Hollo! Thingumbob again!' This implies recognition of essential features of a previous experience, and inductive grouping of the two experiences and some kind of rationalisation of the operation. The 'electric sense of analogy' signals inductive learning by equivalence grouping. Jerome Bruner, whose work we will discuss later, argued that learning is a process by which we

83

structure the world, but it is a process conditioned (for better and for worse) by our own personality and cultural background. We, as inheritors of a Newtonian culture, expect Nature to produce truths as things or relations which exist within it. Science (and common sense) invent ways of grouping these truths. Educational learning is thus, rather lyrically seen by Bruner as a voyage on enchanted seas seeking islands of truth. When we make our discovery landfall we are satisfied if our intuitive structuring of the observable data produces workable and useful discriminations and distinctions. We think this way, Bruner argues, because we have no option, psychologically speaking. We have no other way to work.

In suggesting inductive, 'discovery' learning as the best educational climate in which to consider native language work in schools we can make a tentative, but exciting link between our methods and some of the work which has been carried out in 'cognitive' psychology in recent years, establishing 'discovery' as a stratagem of learning of considerable interest. Whether these experimental findings are wholly relevant to mother-tongue learning situations is not explicitly known, but the position we adopt is an optimistic one. We would not like to think that language learning is wholly separated from any other kind of learning. On the contrary, we would be happy to assert that all other learning is in some way language bound; therefore, stratagems effective in native language learning might be reflected in other experimental learning fields. The work of Katona (1940) and Hendrix (1947), for example, tested the respective merits of memorisation and discovery learning of simple geometrical puzzles (Katona) and established that 'self-help' pupils — i.e. pupils who worked out their own solutions — were more effective in memorisation and transfer than pupils who were given expository rules to help them. Katona suggested that 'formulation of the general principle in words is not indispensable for achieving application'.

Hendrix stated similar findings in a clearer way. 'Groups that discovered the principle independently and left it unverbalised exceeded those who discovered the principle then verbalised it, and both exceeded in transfer those who had the principle stated for them and then illustrated.' Both papers dealt to some extent with the problem of *einstellung*, or mechanical rigidity of learning produced by rules, which impedes applications of the learning. But both provide principles on which the case for discovery learning may be taken forward.

The early work on learning by discovery, that is, work between 1940 and 1960, produced a number of useful dictums which were substantiated by clinical experiments, and which might be thought of as principles of discovery learning. We have already noted Katona's conclusions on 'self-help' being superior and Hendrix's interesting suggestion that an *unverbalised* awareness is more effective in learning than a verbalised awareness. Haselrud and Meyers (1958) gave us two useful dictums as a result of their work; one, that fast learning under guidance was no guarantee of transfer; two, that maturity affects the learning and transfer potential of learning. The first suggestion would appear to argue that no memorisation drills, mnemonics, or rote work are of any use to the learner unless they form the basis of personal discovery. The typical 'fast learning' of the cramming school, or the class work we have all sometimes indulged in as a last minute preparation for public examinations, according to this finding produce only the most superficial learning. The second notion, of maturity and discovery being linked, will recommend itself to most teachers as a partial vindication of Piaget's notion of readiness. Cognitive growth brings children into successive stages of potential learning, where previous learning and developed capacity contribute towards effective discovery. What is crudely called transfer of training thus depends not merely on the teaching technique used, nor on the method behind the techniques, but on the stage of development of the learner.

In at least one important way, school teaching of any subject, English included, consists in intelligently assisting the pupil's own discoveries. The notion that a learner may be guided towards discovery has been investigated by several psychologists. There is some confliction in the results obtained. Craig (1953, 1956) suggested that the more guidance the learner received, the more efficient his discovery would be; the more efficient learning, the more effective would be the transfer. Craig was perfectly logical therefore in claiming that the principles of the solutions to problems in school learning should be stated for the pupil's guidance before the problem is itself tackled. Many teachers would feel, I think, that this is dangerously like expository teaching, without the benefit of the dictated proof. In terms of, say, a grammar lesson, it would be like a statement of grammar without examples, when the pupil has been asked to make an analysis of a text. We would do well to remember that Craig's experimental subjects were (as they are unfortunately in so many psychology experiments) college students. A maturational factor

must surely have played an important part in the 'guided discovery' he described.

It rings much more true to experience to say that too much
direction inhibits learning, rather than advances it. This was the
'middle-of-the-road' position taken up by Kittel (1957) after
a series of experiments on discovery learning. Too little direction
failed to exploit the discovery, he argued, but an 'intermediate'
amount was significantly superior to the two extremes. His subjects were sixth grade school pupils. There is much we would
like clarified here, if the findings are to be of practical use. For
instance, how much is 'too much', how little is 'too little' and
where does the superior 'intermediate' point lie? As it stands, the
advice sounds rather like 'moderation in all things', hardly a
clear-cut basis for syllabus reform.

The question of how a teacher actually handles guidance in
his 'discovery' teaching (that is, teaching which is intended to
produce discovery learning) is interestingly handled by Della-
Piana (1957). He studied the way manipulation of 'feed-back'
to the learner affected his approach to the lesson material. For
example, he showed that the learner who was deprived of simple
signs of encouragement by the teacher, and from a comparison
with the standard progress of the group he was learning in, set
up a 'searching' attitude. In this search, the pupils tended to turn
to the experimenter (or the teacher) for guidance. We may see
this as an anxiety state, albeit one which fruitfully affects motiva-
tion in learning. But it has obvious links with actual teaching
practice. For instance, negative marking techniques, which have
been loudly condemned (and usually rightly so) may be effective
in producing some form of searching orientation; the open class
lesson during which the teacher exposes pupil error may also
produce a searching state. While the suggestions made by
Della-Piana smack of that kind of linear 'reinforcement' based
on stimulus-response learning theory which makes most teachers
shudder, there is no doubt that at a common sense level some
teachers succeed in making their pupils work well in this way.
The question of what we do when the pupil does set up a search
remains critical, however.

Two other pieces of work might be worthy of some consideration here. Kersh's (1962) paper studied the learning which
took place in arithmetic lessons under two different types of
direction. One group was given a thorough course on how the
rule itself was formed (rule learners); another was directed to
the observable patterns of the quantities the problems themselves

showed (discovery learners). These were set against a group which learned by rote the processes involved in the arithmetic studied (rote learners). He found that at the outset of learning, the rote learners were at least as good as the discovery group, and were markedly better than the rule learners. In terms of retention, discovery was superior to rote or to rule, and in transfer or application of the principles, discovery was much superior to rote, but rule learners fell somewhere between the extremes. It might well seem to teachers of English that consideration of papers dealing with arithmetic is irrelevant to questions of language learning. But we should pause before taking too crude a standpoint on this issue. Mathematics is among other things, a rationalisation of experience. The universe is reduced to order, as Andrews said (see Chapter 2). Descriptive work in language study also reduces a world of experience to order. In the past, and in more than one place at present, the debate on the status of the rule of grammar and its relationship to language work in schools has been conducted vigorously. Questions like these are asked: would a course on the making of a simple phrase structure grammar add to pupil insights in language work? Is a rationalistic basis of language description (like TG. See Chapter 3.3) more likely to be profitable for schoolwork than a descriptive standpoint? These questions, at that level of abstraction are decidedly similar to Kersh's, and the possibility of common problems existing between mathematics syllabus reform and that of language teaching cannot be ignored.

Wittrock (1963) carried out work in some way similar to Kersh's. He taught college students to decipher codes, and his methods were these: (1) He gave rule and answer to one group (2) He gave rule, but not answer to a second group (3) He gave the answer only to a third group (4) He gave neither rule nor answer to the fourth group. The most effective *initial* learning came from group (1) ; the least effective *initial* learning came from those with minimum direction, i.e. (4) ; the best conditions for *long-term learning* came from the 'intermediate direction' groups, (2) and (3).

The distinction between learning conditions for initial and long-term use is a just and valuable one, and Kittell, Kersh and Wittrock agree in principle on intermediate direction being the most effective teaching technique in discovery. But it highlights the need for us to specify accurately our learning goals in thinking about method and technique. Parts of the English syllabus may be well handled by initial fast learning, for example

87

necessary technicalities of verse form, of punctuation and of spelling, while other parts may need learning which produces the maximum relevance to the pupil in terms of retention and transfer characteristics. 'When the criterion of learning is initial learning of a few responses, explicit and detailed direction seems to be the most effective and efficient. When the criteria of learning are retention and transfer, some intermediate amount of direction seems to produce the best results' (Wittrock, 1963).

No discussion of this field of educational psychology would be complete without a consideration of the contribution of J. S. Bruner. For most teachers his work stands out as the most readable and most stimulating writing in the field of learning theory. Bruner's *The Process of Education* (1960) is studied by many students during their teacher training and of his many other works, his contribution to *Studies in Cognitive Growth* (1965) has stimulated much fruitful discussion and some research in the field of language learning. His debt to Piaget is expressed clearly in his *Process* (1960) where he drew attention to the importance of *structure* in learning, to the concept of *readiness* to learn, to the nature and value of *intuition* in school learning, and to the place of *interest* in the process of education. The edge and style of Bruner's arguments may be gauged from his statement in 1960 that any subject can be taught effectively in some intellectually honest form to any child at any stage of his development. This statement is not anarchic; quite the reverse. It shows the importance in syllabus formation of our knowing as much as possible about the development of the child's mind, about our subject and about the method by which we promote learning.

Bruner does not slavishly follow Piaget's stages of readiness, which most teachers will remember were the pre-operational, the stage of concrete operations, and the stage of formal operations. Bruner's terms propose a somewhat different emphasis on readiness: *enactive*, *iconic* and *symbolic*. This classification of mental development offers a concept structure by which teachers may devise approaches and grade materials for use at different stages of growth. Bruner's notion that the youngest school learner operates principally by acting in and on his environment might well be taken as a re-statement of the basis of nursery and infant educational practice. His hypothesis that children from about six to eleven years of age learn effectively by a vivid process of analogy again rings true to experience. In the child's most advanced stage he thinks like an adult and becomes capable of calculation and symbolic operations (such as analysis, synthesis, deduction, etc.) and he argues that the child in this stage not only has the capacity to think in this abstract way, but has a mental need to carry out calculation and manipulation of this sort. The underlying notion of stages of learning puts educational interpretation on the Pauline remark 'When I was a child, I spake as a child, I understood as a child: but when I became a man, I put away childish things.'

As we quoted earlier, one of the most fertile of Bruner's suggestions was that learning was a way of structuring the world, and that this process is conditioned by our cultural and personality background. Bruner's point, that we are *obliged* to think like this, psychologically, argues the necessity of teachers thinking in terms of the structure of learning in a language syllabus. That is to say, the syllabus must be geared to individuals forming for themselves effective learning structures in their own discoveries. In his later work (1965) and in several other places, Bruner refers to this structuring in terms of 'codes'. In his view, what is often thought of inaccurately as specific transfer of training is better interpreted as the presence or absence in the learning of effective coding devices. Thus, how we structure a piece of learning will colour how we recognise similarities and differences in later learning situations. In this he recalls Spearman's principles (1923) whose work on the 'education of correlates' forms a basis of much recent thinking on cognition. Bruner interprets Spearman's point in this way: that going beyond the information given in learning is the most important characteristic of human mental life (1957). He takes the question of colour discrimination as an example (it is also an interesting semantic problem). If there are 7·5 million discriminable colours, physically speaking, it is surely significant that human language manages to operate with only a dozen or so categories. There must therefore be a highly effective coding of colour by which we structure experience. Bruner argues that the probability texture of experience enters into our learning and helps us to go beyond the information given in any situation, and to form codes which structure reality for us, making it manipulable and memorable.

The coding ability makes us think carefully about language itself. If it is merely a set of chains of words or phrases, describable as a Markov series, we would be obliged to assume that the mind was only a simple switching machine with two states, one ON and one OFF. Therefore in a language, like English or any other living language, where there is for all practical purposes an infinite variety of ways in which sentences may be varied, we would have to assume that the brain was capable of making an infinite number of switching judgements. Similarly, in vision, if we assume that we 'construct' or 'create' the patterns that make up the visual world from a simple chain of on/off responses to stimuli, we would fail to account for the way the human viewer sees the world in patterns. There is a coding device in vision by which the brain makes finite visionary sense out of what is an infinite possibility of sight; similarly, in language there is a coding device in the human mind which allows the speaker to make sentences useful for communication – understandable correct sentences – and which allows him to decode communicable sentences from the infinite possibility of heard speech noise. The argument is that in language, and probably in all human cognition, there must be abstract mechanisms, which are not able to be analysed in terms of simple reflex association, or chains of stimuli and responses, but which are continually and creatively in use in our thinking.

This is the more technical interpretation of 'codes', but Bruner and others have put a more practical gloss on the term also. They have discussed the conditions under which the pupil's intuitions of grouping may be given a chance to come into free play in the learning situation. They have rightly stressed interest as a factor; they have urged that pupils faced with lesson materials should be given liberty to react and to express themselves; they have urged the adoption of intuitively acceptable groupings as the most likely to be fertile in the class learning situation.

Clearly, in any syllabus in language which attempts to make the language environment of the child rational and articulate, we must give considerable thought to the kind of language description we employ. Ideally, the pupils, after suitable exposure to a wide range of texts should themselves propose a description. Sweet advocated this over a hundred years ago; it is by no means a recent idea. Perhaps in syllabuses dedicated to excluding formal grammar of any sort each pupil does create for himself a manipulable coding device, and a description which serves him well in rationalising his natural reaction to texts. If a personal grammar acts in this way as a heuristic device in language work, however, it would surely be eminently reasonable to help the pupil towards a description which would form the basis of group discussion about the nature of texts, and more, would form a basis of understanding in some way the nature of language in general. Bruner and many of his psychological colleagues have readily adopted Chomsky's generative grammar as the basis of such a description. There is undoubtedly a powerful urge to do this in academic psycholinguistic research. Chomsky's linguistic theory is highly fashionable; it is mathematical and lends itself to certain interesting computational techniques in research; it has itself become, in recent years, both a theory of language and a theory of mind (see Chomsky, 1968b). This use of transformational generative linguistics by psychology should not be interpreted as an out and out rejection of 'positivistic' or objective approaches to language description, where these can be shown to be useful. Bruner's reference to the need for 'categories' and 'sub-assemblies' in his latest major work would seem to indicate this. Further, no respectable educational psychologist would like to ally himself with a linguistic theory which is itself fragmentary, and in flux. As we have seen in our discussion of initial acquisition of the mother-tongue, mainline TG has proved itself unacceptable to at least one major child language project (Edinburgh) because of its weakness in semantics, especially related to meaning in situation.

# 7 Rhetoric in a New Key

There are two main lines of force detectable in the English language courses we have come to describe as 'traditional'. One of these is rhetoric; the other is the study of grammar. In a certain sense both have been eclipsed by recent trends in language teaching. Rhetoric, which teachers will remember best in its recent form of lists of figures of speech to be identified in literary texts, has largely disappeared from the objective study of texts in school; grammar, as we have argued at length elsewhere in this book, has either suffered a rejection fit for the plague, or has survived in an entrenched and crystallised form in the course-books which lie in the cupboards of many a schoolroom. Yet one has only to look at developments in the English syllabus in schools to discover that a profound awareness of the social role of language exists in the classroom. Teachers and pupils investigate appropriate and inappropriate ways of speaking and writing; the intention of authors is studied to establish irony, sarcasm, parody; the source and format of English texts are studied; free writing explores styles, and, in brief, a whole climate of interest in the varieties of language is encountered. It appears that certain valuable features of the older kinds of rhetoric have survived the outdated rhetorical methods our schools inherited. Approaches to style, appropriateness of text or varieties of language are more and more being linked with some form of linguistic description of texts. In this way rhetoric has re-entered the classroom, albeit in a new key.

The study of rhetoric, which flowered in our universities, particularly the universities of Scotland, until the early decades of this century, was largely a by-product of the study of classical literature. Since the study of English in the nineteenth century in England and Scotland was significantly under the control of the classicists – often with the classics master teaching English – it is not surprising to find that the approaches to the criticism of the language of texts, to the nature of error and to the work of composition in English were much influenced by the principles of rhetoric. In Scotland, we can see the influence of two main groups of rhetoricians in the formative nineteenth century, a group centred round Campbell (1776) (including Kames, 1762 and Blair, 1783) and a group more loosely associated with Bain (1869, 1887) which included DeQuincey. We might thrust Grierson into association with Bain because he was Bain's junior colleague and successor in rhetoric at Aberdeen. This would obscure the fact that Grierson, who published his well known book *Rhetoric and English Composition* as late as 1944, was a man of modern textual criticism, who made many suggestions about rhetoric which link directly with much that linguistics has said in recent years about language variety study.

How did these rhetoricians describe their science? Campbell defined rhetoric in a sentence drawn from Cicero: 'Rhetoric is the art or talent by which discourse is adapted to its end.' Methodologically, he treated rhetoric as if it operated on two planes. On the one hand he regarded it as a speculative enquiry into the laws of universal literature, and on the other, as a technique for the practical criticism of texts, and thereby, by implication, as a practical guide to the art of composition. This dual role given to rhetoric interestingly reflects something of the double aim given to Latin grammar in mediaeval education. After the rediscovery of the grammar and rhetoric of Aristotle, together with Jewish and Arab commentaries on the works, Latin grammar was taught both as a practical tool to aid reading and as a branch of speculative philosophy.[1]

The climate of idealism which prevailed in nineteenth-century education seems to have blurred the distinction between these goals. Teachers appeared to think (and some still do today) that it was reasonable that a body of academic knowledge, justified by scholars, should both be the content of a school course and should provide a practical method for composition. Education in the nineteenth century, of course, felt that it was dedicated to excellence, albeit an excellence which might only exist as a golden rule. Rhetoric (and grammar) provided the rules by which excellence might be attained, or, more usually, provided the teachers with a means of detecting and measuring error. This kind of 'excellence' is dedicated to making pupils' efforts seem to fall short; it promotes prescription of the worst kind, and it fosters doctrines of 'correctness' with all their complications of critical and social priggishness; in its approach to texts, either through the means of rhetoric or grammar, this excellence is rule-centred rather than usage-centred and tended to make all diachronic (or progressive historical) changes of language seem pejorative.

The result of this view of rule-bound writing is well known. Writing as a direct expression of a pupil's own ideas virtually stopped. For example, the inhibition of student writing reached an extreme under Bain, who forbade the writing of essays by university students on the grounds that bricks could not be made without straw. Since students appeared not to know the principles of rhetoric, Bain concluded that they could not safely be asked to write English. Interestingly enough this inhibition was not restricted to universities and schools. Martin (1961) shows that the dearth of imaginative fiction in America in the early nineteenth century can be directly related to the effect of Scottish rhetoric and philosophy applied (or misapplied) with idealistic fervour.

Campbell believed profoundly that principles were prior to practice and superior to practice. Yet, rather interestingly, in a book describing the principles of composition, he finds it necessary to apologise for the style he has written in. 'Nor can anything be further from (the author's) thoughts than to pretend to an exemption from such positive faults in expression as, in the article of elocution, he hath freely criticised in the best English authors.' Is it possible that Campbell, knowing the principles of elegance, intentionally wrote in a faulty style, or is it not more likely that his own body of rhetorical rules was ideal, and inevitably criticised as inferior whatever was practical? One is reminded of excellent Greek warriors who always felt themselves to be inferior to the gods.

The contradiction between principles and performance in writing infected the schools of the nineteenth century and the pre-occupation with error which gripped education is not entirely out of our classrooms yet. Teachers did not, apparently, suspect that there might be a philosophical flaw in the link between principles and performance when they found that children could know their grammar (or rhetoric) and still perform lamentably in productive composition work or in the perceptive criticism of texts. Craik, the Senior Chief Inspector of the Scottish Education Department, writing his annual reports of 1895 and 1900 made typical complaints of this order. Struthers, his successor, made similar remarks in 1907 and 1913. A whole range of school textbooks of the last and present century have, in their prefaces, remarks about the urgent need for more work on principles to produce more and better performance in the language. The rhetorical movement embraced a simplistic idea of transfer from principle to practice which the schools, through the work of Campbell, Bain and others accepted as authoritative.

Bain was not only a university rhetorician, he was a writer of school textbooks and he had considerable influence in America as well as in Britain. He believed that it was 'a possible thing to arrive at a definite code of prescriptions for regulating the Intellectual Qualities of Composition' (1869). These 'Intellectual Qualities' included syntax as well as style. He suggested that these prescriptions should form both a discipline for schools and a practical teaching model for writing. In this he clearly perpetuated the split goal we have noted in Campbell.

It is important to notice that Campbell and Bain both tried, as far as possible, to use the principles of rhetoric as part of the wide reading of literature. They may have adopted a method we disapprove of, but the idea of having pupils read widely and talk sensibly about the way the texts are written is still advocated in schools today, and indeed, it forms one of the new directions stressed in the publications of the Scottish Central Committee on English (1967, 1968) – that principles of description ought to be implied by texts and demonstrated from living literature rather than learned as detached drills or exercises.

Although it is clear that Bain knew the distinctions between grammatical form and rhetorical style, he is not at all clear in his exposition of the differences. He was highly prescriptive in his approach to texts, and his favourite occupation seemed to be re-casting the English of the Authorised Version of the Bible to give it greater clarity and effect. 'Easy is my yoke, and light is my burden' is one proposal for example. He had no time for performance irregularities in language, the idiomatic roughnesses, the time-honoured phrases in which so much of the life of the spoken language lies. Ambiguity was abhorrent to him, and he may be seen in this as a scholar of the temper of Donatus who was not content to find evidence for the best Latin in the universally accepted 'best' authors of his own literature, but who criticised the sacrosanct and irreproachable Virgil for his offences against grammar and style. This dangerous and alluring precedent, as Wattie has called it (1930), has been widely followed in approaches to English in our own time.

Grierson was the student and, later from 1897, the junior colleague of Bain. In many ways he is an apologist for Bain to a century which began to doubt the value of idealistic approaches in education, first in mathematics and science and latterly in other fields. Grierson lectured early, from the nineties, but published during the second world war. His *Rhetoric and English Composition* (1944) shows him to be the bringer of two new in-

95

fluences into the teaching of rhetoric. First of all, he re-fertilised existing rhetorical theory by a re-discovery of the *Rhetoric* of Aristotle, a work which had been somewhat neglected since Campbell's day because of the strong Platonic climate in philosophy and education in the nineteenth century. Secondly, Grierson is a modern flexible thinker, much more empirical than any of his predecessors. Bain would seem to have, like Plato, inscribed above the gate of his academy 'Let none ignorant of geometry (or rhetoric) enter here'. Grierson is much more concerned with a liberal reaction to texts and is descriptively orientated to the style.

Grierson gave as his definition of rhetoric 'the study of how to express oneself correctly and effectively, bearing in mind the nature of the language we use, the subject we are speaking or writing about, the kind of audience we have in view (often only vaguely definable), and the purpose, which last is the main determinant'. This might well have been a preliminary definition of style used by a descriptive linguist in much more recent years.

He set out in his rhetoric certain principles, some relating to grammar and syntax, some to vocabulary, some to the handling of subjects and in addition he made some remarkable statements about the relationship between a speaker and his audience from the point of view of persuading people to accept the subject matter spoken about. One feels that Grierson is attacking Bain's prescriptivism when he urges us to guard against the error of laying down non-English prescriptions for English writing — which is what many rules of rhetoric and grammar had become. Grammar, he claimed, does not prescribe laws for a language, but exists to ascertain and define the usage of those who are regarded as speaking the language well. Thus, grammar becomes a descriptive instrument and a heuristic device. Neither Campbell nor Bain would have accepted this. This so deflates the idea that grammar is principle that it questions the basis of the nineteenth-century view, and the eighteenth before it, that grammar and rhetoric were based on universal principles which were prescriptive and inviolable, and that performance changes must necessarily be produced by a mastery of these principles.

Linguistics itself has, of course, since Grierson's time moved from a phase of criticism (rejection) of universal rules of grammar and phonology into a rationalist phase in which the theory of universals is again acceptable. But we should not confuse the notion of 'universal rule' of grammar when it is proposed as part of a practical course of writing with the notion of a universal in linguistic theory where the concept is explanatory within the rationalisation of the theory. A rule of writing is concerned with performance in writing, with the actual language produced on a given occasion, while the universal in linguistic theory is concerned with giving a satisfactory explanation of what might be said to underlie our abilities to produce, organise and understand sentences. Chomsky is attempting to understand 'that part of psychology which is referred to as linguistics' (see *Language and Mind*, 1968) ; Bain and his schoolmaster disciples are concerned with legislating for the performance of language, providing a 'machine' in the form of rules which makes language seem uncreative and crude.

Grierson's imaginative proposals for rhetoric did not much affect the schools, except through the individual efforts of his university students of the thirties (Edinburgh) who were very much inspired by his lectures. The late publication of his small book (1944) together with the second world war effectively scotched any direct effect on the syllabus. It was only in the fifties and early sixties, in Scotland particularly, when a fresh review of the syllabus began to take place, that an interest in the study of varieties of language arose offering Grierson's ideas scope in schools. In our view this was a call for rhetoric with a new emphasis. Since the late fifties it has been answered in part by linguistic studies of 'register', but these have not proved entirely satisfactory, as we shall see below.

One of the principal points made by linguists is that language is, like mathematics, 'peculiar among systems, in that it abuts on reality in two places instead of one'. (Joos.) Language has formal meaning and situational meaning. All language is part of a wide non-language situation, and in most cases a language utterance could be thought of as a small part of the total situation. One of the interests of linguistics in the last two decades has been the description of how the language of an utterance links with the meaning of the situation. Firth's view was that both form and context were modes of meaning and it was principally from a semantic viewpoint that he proposed (after Malinowski) a description of 'register' or, in other terms, of language variety related to language use. A definition current in register studies is, '*Register* is the general term used for the varieties of language, or sets of language patterning obtained by relating situational and linguistic groupings' (Ure, 1965). Several other definitions follow this one closely usually referring to the correlation between 'types of situation and types of utterance'. Clearly, this

97

enquiry, although first thought of in terms of purely linguistic distinctions, is an enquiry into part of the field our predecessors would have called rhetoric.

Before you can talk about varieties of language being meaningful in different situations you must assume a single, whole language (*une langue une* as Saussure called it). Catford (1965), Gregory (1967) and others have pointed out that the concept of a 'whole language' is not an operationally possible idea. It is best to regard varieties as sub-languages of some order. Catford advocated classifying the *user's* variations, proposing a kind of idiolectal study – 'dialect' in its broadest, and yet its most personal sense. Other linguists have concentrated on the *use* as a means of sub-classifying the language, and some of the best known exponents of register studies have advocated this, Spencer and Gregory (1964), Gregory (1967), Halliday *et al.* (1964). In general the use of the word 'register' implies this latter view – that use is the key to sub-classification of language variety. Both approaches run into a series of semantic difficulties in dealing with situation. It is indisputable that we cannot completely describe situation, but our inability to describe it fully should not prevent us from describing it at all.

*Situation* is the term we use to cover the non-language part of the whole setting of an utterance. It is the place, the speaker and hearer, the time, the cause of the speech and, in short, all the parts of the total situation except those identifiably within language. In grappling with the notion of situation we are very much faced with the problem of clothing the universality of situation with manipulable and relevant categories. It is rather like Ullmann's point (1962) that mankind has taken the spectrum and categorised it into groups of wavelengths which we call colours. The problem for education and linguistics is identifying from the totality of situation aspects or categories of situation which are relevant to the study of the meaning of utterances. Firth has proposed a 'context of situation' in which all the non-language features relevant to the meaning of an utterance are contained. This itself raises a problem of selection for a given utterance. Clearly there are many aspects of situation which are highly relevant to the meaning of an utterance; there are some which are less urgently relevant, and some which are only marginally relevant – to take only three points on the continuum of relevance. Lyons (1963) takes up a point of view basically similar to Firth's, but more exhaustively defined, if also more abstractly treated. He points out that both speaker and hearer, the events and objects and 'various factors and features relating to these objects and events' and to be taken into account in defining relevant situational meaning. This very broad definition does not help teachers much in their task of reducing the notion of context of situation to workable dimensions. For pedagogical reasons we are obliged to be reasonably coarse in our classifications of situation relevant to the utterance.

Halliday (*et al.*) (1964) proposes a workable classification of varieties related to only three main categories of language use : 'Registers . . . may be distinguished according to field of discourse, mode of discourse and style of discourse' (1964:90). In general this tripartite division of situation is accepted by Spencer and Gregory (1964) although they are, quite reasonably, worried by the term 'style' as one feature of variety, when, clearly, the lay use of the term and educated literary use of the word imply the whole field of variety. Spencer and Gregory also reject 'genre' as a synonym and propose 'tenor'. Thus, *field* of discourse, *mode* of discourse and *tenor* of discourse are proposed in Spencer and Gregory's useful, early book in this area of study. It may seem odd to teachers to be told that these terms are linguistic categories and they refer respectively to situational categories of *subject matter*, degree of *colloquiality*, and degree of *formality* in personal relationships. It may well be that this proposal for two sets of parallel terms, one linguistic and one extra-linguistic, indicates that in the fifties and early sixties, before the revival of interest in semantics overtook linguistic study in general, those who studied 'register' were at pains to show that varieties were shown *linguistically* to be distinctive. Thus considerable weight was given to a study of forms and frequencies of forms in descriptive linguistic terms, and these were correlated with the outer darkness of situation by way of 'parameters' which showed how language forms correlated with intuitively classified situational features of utterance. A high degree of respectability was held to be produced by 'linguistic' means of differentiating varieties – numbers of passives used, distribution of embedded as opposed to non-embedded clauses and the like. The changing grammars of linguistics largely made 'register' studies obsolete before they had any wide effects. I suspect there was also a great deal of dissatisfaction in school circles because the terminology of this linguistically orientated study of style was esoteric. One often discovered a teacher much excited by the possibility of reviving study of language variety in class either happily misusing the terms, or obliging his pupils to learn abstract new terms like 'genre' without any supporting understanding of what it was all about. On the other hand, common sense has a way of asserting itself in the English class. It is part of our own linguistic tradition to be aware that different forms of language have different effects; equally, that different forms of language may be used to secure the same effects. Before they were really aware of the theoretical status of 'deep' grammar, teachers were happily relating underlying networks of systems in linguistics, like mood, transitivity, etc., to their realisations in utterances and to their effects in language use. They did this because it is intuitively and culturally acceptable to us to believe that our language does have resources of form and does have effects on situation which we can categorise in some way. In even more recent terms, we could say that teachers realised that under the surface utterance of language lie the networks of relationships which give the utterance formal meaning, and under the deep systems (networks) lie the sociolinguistic relationships of man speaking to man. Halliday has suggested that person-to-person relationships give entry to deep linguistic systems, which are in turn realised as a string of language forms in the utterance. This utterance in turn is heard, decoded in terms of its surface elements, and their relationships at the deep level appreciated and finally the message of social relationships between speaker and hearer is known. This socio-linguistic cycle characterises the position most teachers find they have adopted intuitively in their approach to varieties and styles.[2]

One of the distinctions made by workers in 'register' studies (particularly clearly made by Miss Jean Ure, 1965) is that where the teaching is of English as a second language, the concentration should be on the positive description of linguistic aspects of variety and their relationship(s) with a definable social situation, but where the teaching was designed for native speakers intuitive responses to variety could be used. There is some justice in this remark. Native speakers have a native social environment and that implies that people in general agree on the meaning of utterances. For example jokes on national television exploit a common sense of the ridiculous; orders are orders everywhere and to everybody in the mother-tongue area; persuasion is on a common basis; exhortation likewise (happily for salesmen and politicians) is based on a common socio-linguistic sense. In short there is a wealth of common understanding of the wider meaning of utterances in a native-speaking environment which

100

cannot be presumed in many second language environments. One is very reluctant to accept this as an either/or principle for teachers however. There are certain universal features of language in use which make cross-cultural intuitions possible. This is more true of European languages like English and French, or English and German than of links between English and African languages, which Miss Ure refers to. For instance German advertisers make use of manipulations of graphology which recall those used in Britain. This would argue an appeal to a common set of reactions to language use, at least at a basic level. In principle my argument is that we cannot view languages as entirely separate from each other in terms of their varieties. Thus we should not automatically assume that any EFL or ESL situation implied non-continuity between the 'common senses' about language in each country. Further, the interest in phonological and other linguistic universals, fostered in the latest phase of study of generative grammars, may well add theory to support our impressions on this aspect of continuity between languages and cultures.

Grierson took up an Aristotelian view of rhetoric, concerning himself with the speaker, his subject and his audience. Modern linguistic approaches are similar. Lyons discussed one aspect of this in glossing his use of the term 'context' (1963:83); 'The context of the utterance must be held to include, not only the relevant external objects and the actions taking place at the time, but the knowledge shared by the speaker and the hearer of all that has gone before . . .'. In particular, the context of a sentence in a written work must be understood to include the conventions governing the literary genre of which the work in question is an example. Further, Lyons argues that context also includes 'the tacit acceptance by the speaker and hearer of all the relevant conventions, beliefs and presuppositions "taken for granted" by members of the speech community to which the speaker and the hearer belong' (1963: 413). This is a very important issue for the description of language variety. What the speaker knows, latently or otherwise, about his language, and what the hearer knows, contribute significantly to the nature of persuasion, of description, of evocation, etc. Grierson put it slightly differently when he proposed that the art of persuasion consisted partly in appealing to what the hearer half believed already. A linguistic approach to rhetoric must propose what aspects of utterance are 'taken for granted' by both parties, and what features of language an audience (or a reader or hearer) are predisposed to, already aware of, or 'know' latently, and would draw on in the two-way traffic of persuasion through a text.

We should remember that the conventions referred to as 'in the speaker and hearer's background' are not restricted to literary ones. Non-art conventions in journalistic text and advertising copy are equally open to analysis on the basis of what speakers or hearers 'know' already, and these conventions are coarsely similar to those of literature in that they are recognised intuitively and are restricted by certain linguistic circumscriptions which are describable, such as range of alphabets, intonation patterns, vocabulary and accents (Leech, 1964). Thus, what Grierson (and Aristotle) postulated on a non-linguistic basis can be clarified by linguistics. The question we must try to answer with the help of linguistics is this, 'What features of their own common language do speakers and hearers (or writers and readers) bring to the fashioning and interpretation of varieties of the mother-tongue?' This question is neither strictly user-based (like idiolect) nor use-based, but spans both considerations. Our approach to rhetoric from this angle, outlined below, and in more detail in Chapter 8, is specifically related to the shaping of a school course in English language where native speakers form the bulk of the pupils.

*Intention* was the key to traditional rhetoric. Campbell, for instance, held 'purpose' to be the main factor in style, rhetoric being the 'art . . . by which discourse is adapted to its end'. Grierson spells out that 'purpose (which glosses our term "intention") . . . is the main determinant' (1944:24). In vulgar terms, we ask of texts, 'What does the author/speaker want his text to do?' Sometimes in class we put it this way: 'Why should he write it this way?' The focus of each question can be altered to deal with phonological, or graphological features of the text, to draw attention to features of form, of vocabulary selection and juxtaposition, and to issues of context. In practice we begin by thinking about the wider aspects of a text as a socio-linguistic phenomenon, by asking questions about *source*. Source and intention are closely bound up together. Source investigates where a text might have been found in use in the business of our normal lives – newspapers, advertising copy, a poem, play or television script, etc. – and it exploits commonsense knowledge of the world children live in. Intention follows from source (when one is critically examining a text) since where and how a text is used gives us a very good indication of what the author wanted to achieve by publishing it. From the author's point of view, intention precedes all the other aspects of style. It is the notional basis on which the whole creative act of communication rests.

Clearly the study of style can be regarded in several very different ways. In one light, style may be seen as a kind of efficiency test applied to texts, and by implication, to authors. The nineteenth century was all too fond of detecting errors of style. Bain, as we have noted, was much taken up with this, and his coursebooks contain 'promiscuous exercises' in which a random selection of errors was presented to the scholar for his correction in the light of the rules of style. Rhetoricians of Bain's day took it upon themselves to purge literature of error, and the enthusiasm with which this was done carried some to nonsensical lengths. Some grammarians like Cobbett (1826) argued tenaciously that they would not hear precedents drawn from Milton, Johnson, Watts, the King, aristocrats and others because these writers were in breach of grammar; some rhetoricians like De Quincey (1860) held the remarkable view that there was hardly a page of the fairest writers of their day that was not suspect in some aspect of its grammar or style. We can safely dismiss these attitudes to grammar and style in today's schools as being totally unrepresentative of the empirical spirit with which we approach the modern world. What Grierson said of Aristotle is true of us: *he approached rhetoric as a man of science, not for what ought to be, but for what is.*

It is interesting to note the link that exists between a notionally based rhetoric, such as the one we are proposing, and some recent work in linguistics. In a systemic grammar a network of dependencies is said to lie under the utterances we make; these dependencies and other relationships may be informally characterised semantically as choices, for example in the mood system as choices such as 'Is there a *command* or not; if not, is there a *question* or not?' Teachers will recognise much of the notional approach of traditional grammar in this, even if the choice framework proposed is far more extensive than any suggested by traditional linguistics. More interestingly, the notion that all these underlying choice systems are the process of socio-linguistic choices of speaker role, of purpose, of agency, goal, etc., suggests that at least one important modern grammatical approach is grappling with language in terms of rhetoric.[3]

A socio-linguistic view of rhetoric concerns itself with the *intention* of a text (or utterance), with the *form* of the utterance and with the *social relationships* produced by the language with

103

regard to the participants. In dealing with these three areas of interest we should remember that they are selected aspects of discourse and in no sense exhaustively define discourse features. Further, they are not mutually exclusive areas; intention may reveal itself in form; form can indicate such matters as degree of colloquiality, dialect features, etc., and these will in turn link with the relationships of people involved in the discourse. Again, we are perfectly happy to approach distinctions of style from either the non-language end (e.g. what subjects are being discussed, who is speaking, where, etc.) or from the formal end (occurrence of passives, reduced forms of verbs, hesitation phenomena, etc.). In short, taking up Halliday's dictum that all linguistics is socio-linguistics, one would look on every text studied in a school context as a sample of man speaking to man; whether we begin from a recognisably social context for our enquiry into texts, or from a more formal viewpoint of the structure of language matters little. The important factor is that linguistic structure and social structure are closely related to each other and a modern view of rhetoric has the responsibility of asserting this in articulate terms.

Some very interesting areas of socio-linguistics have been explored in recent years and together these throw light on rhetoric. For example, Bernstein (1965) has explored the idea of 'speech-codes'. He pointed out that language may take the form of an *elaborated* or a *restricted* code dependent on the social relationships obtaining between the participants. A style involving an elaborated code, the syntax and vocabulary likely to be used by the speaker cannot easily be predicted. It is flexible, resourceful and highly tailored to fit specific subjects and situations. For instance an elaborate and imaginative explanation by a mother to a child on some aspect of behaviour would fall into the category 'elaborated'. In contrast, a mother unwilling or unable to fashion an explanation, but curbing the child's behaviour in some linguistic way, may take the form of a restricted code, in which the mother may repeat brief, non-discursive instructions to the child which brook neither discussion nor verbal response, except of a restricted, protest sort.

In a more detailed way Labov (1966), working on the speech of New Yorkers, has been able to show in detail that a very close relationship exists between social class and both what people say and how they say it. This is a detailed study, and has been matched by others in micro-linguistic studies, but the main message of the work is that we are slowly becoming able to define language and its social, and thereby its stylistic, components in many of its ramifications. Teachers interested in this development should read John Pride's valuable book *The Social Meaning of Language* (1971), which outlines work in the area and summarises much of the research in a very readable way.

If we consider the question of colloquiality in the language of a text some interesting socio-linguistic features of rhetoric emerge. If we can joke that someone 'speaks like a book' we are obviously well aware that there are certain features of utterance which are more characteristic of formal, written texts than of casual, spoken ones. That is putting it in its most parsimonious form. In fact, although there is a clear difference in media between spoken and written language the degree to which spoken forms appear in the conventions of written texts gives us one of the most fruitful areas for describing style linguistically.

Linguists who have concerned themselves with language varieties have made many of their most telling points in dealing with the degree of colloquiality of texts. Spencer and Gregory defined *mode* as 'the dimension (of discourse) which accounts for the linguistic differences which result from the distinction between spoken and written discourse' (1964). Other definitions which substantially agree with this include Bowen (1966) and Ure (1965) where the term used is *medium*. Halliday *et al*. (1964) and Catford (1965) also propose this area as a useful one for the study of 'register'. With so much agreement between scholars, one would expect a crisply defined term to be available for our use, but both *mode* and *medium* are used, confusingly, since medium has already a commonsense meaning for non linguists. To some extent this is also true of *mode*, but, on the grounds that some kind of term is needed, that mode is not wildly confusing and is a welcome relief from 'degree of colloquiality' we adopt it here with Spencer and Gregory's meaning, quoted earlier in this paragraph.

Basic to the distinctions of mode is our view of the relationships which exist between writing and speech. Mode implies more than a distinction of substance, i.e. more than the differences that result from speech being patterns of sounds and writing being patterns of marks. Speech and writing are taken to be semi-independent (and therefore semi-dependent) systems within a language. It is useful to define the relationship between speech and writing in roughly the terms proposed by McIntosh (1961b). He rejects the simple linear view either that writing is a pale reflection of speech or that speech (as the Victorians urged in their rhetoric) was a poor reflection of writing. McIntosh puts forward the Aristotelian view of the three-cornered relationship which exists between mental events, speech and writing. It boils down to a question of encoding. The same mental events may be realised as speech or as writing, and it is perfectly possible within style for what we have written to influence the style of our speech, or *vice versa* for speech forms to influence what we write. Thus a two-way arrow, as it were, should be drawn between speech and writing as systems.

It is reasonable to argue for speech primacy in a historical and a developmental sense, and further to argue, as Abercrombie does (1965) that the letter is basically phonemic in origin ; but it would be wrong to regard writing as a second class utterance system derived from and dependent upon speech. Some scholars take a more extreme view, and regard speech and writing as 'essentially two different languages' (Palmer, 1965). Palmer shows media differences, spelling and related pronunciation differences and grammatical differences. His argument runs like this : some verbs which are regular in speech are not regular in writing, and *vice versa*, he claims, taking *have/has*, *do/does* and *go/goes* as his model. He argues that, in the written language the form *has* is irregular (we would expect *\*haves*) while *does* is regular. In the spoken language *does* /dʌz/ and *has* /hæ z/ are both irregular — /dʌz/ because it alters the vowel of the verb, /hæz/ because it loses a phoneme /v/. A comparison with *go, goes*; *love, loves*, etc., will reveal these differences. He does not leave his case there, of course, but pursues it through the irregularities in speech between positive and negative forms of *can*, *am* and *shall* in terms of their vowels. Further, he makes a telling general point that English has five vowels in its writing system but by no means can we reduce the sound system of the language to less than six.

From the point of view of what we have called *mode* we are interested, among other things, in spelling problems and their relationship with pronunciation. It is more and more the case that texts drawn from modern advertising (and in some cases, modern literature) make striking use of 'phonetic' spelling and achieve a degree of speech effect (DRINKA PINTA MILKA DAY). We might find much more to interest us in the way stress and intonation are indicated in writing. Punctuation is one obvious way in which the conventions of writing make an attempt to reflect the phonology of the utterance, but the conventions of

106

punctuation have seemed a considerable limitation to many styles of writing. Italicisation, choice of a bold letter face, capitalisation of words, underscoring, colour and many additional diacritic symbols have been used in different texts to try to make the written language look somehow more like the spoken. For example, we can 'bend' words to indicate their intonation or stress and thus, often, their meaning.

```
      CIT
 EX    ING !
```

```
             ?
           G
         N
       I
     T
   I
   C
 EX
```

*John* didn't go to the theatre.

John *didn't* go to the theatre.

What we, as teachers, are particularly interested in, however, is the relationship between the spoken and the written, not the exclusion of writing from speech or *vice versa* which is Palmer's aim in his study of the English verb.

One of the most interesting features of mode in a written text is the inclusion in the writing of features which recall the characteristics of spontaneous spoken language. If we think of different kinds of pause in spontaneous speech we will find examples of this. Pause is a salient feature of spontaneous speech utterances and it is a useful marker of degree of colloquiality when it is reflected in writing. An orthographic transcription of conversation might show a rich crop of pauses:

> tell you what happened . . . em . . . last summer which . . .
> eh . . . eh startled me a bit . . . m.eh.n not . . . em . . . not
> being . . . em a native of this part . . . em I've not seen many
> deer . . . and . . . eh when we were walking up this . . .
> eh.eh. the Rinns of Kells em . . . there was a big fence . . .
> you see . . . which we had to cross . . . and as I as we crossed
> it, a deer ran . . . bounding away

107

In this short text there are many filled pauses like . . . *em* . . .
or . . . *eh.eh.* and a smaller number of unfilled pauses marked
merely by . . . . Speculatively we might classify some of the pauses
as associated with lexical search (. . . *em* . . . *last summer;*
. . . *eh.eh.the Rinns of Kells*), some are at expected juncture
points (. . . *em I've not seen many deer* . . . *and* . . . *eh when*)
where a participial phrase (or a minor clause) is separated from
a principal clause and, immediately following this, the linker
*and* between the principal clause and an adverbial clause of time
is associated with pauses before and after the word. A degree of
hesitancy about the selection of a negative (*m.eh.n not* . . . *em*
. . . *not being*) is noted. Many speech transcriptions show the
pause being used as a rejection device as in (*he works at Lloyds
not the* . . . *its the insurance company not the bank*) where the
speaker has rejected a negative structure which would probably
have run to *not the bank but the insurance company* and has
opted for the simple positive declarative structure.

Pause phenomena may in fact give us a clue to the relationship between the underlying notions and the realisation of the
utterance at the surface. In a slightly different sense, as has been
suggested in recent work undertaken by Laver (1969), pauses
may be part of slips of the tongue where inadvertent, but highly
revealing errors in speech take place such as *khandigates* . . .
*candidates*, spoonerisms and other phenomena of this sort.
Again, there is a clear relationship between pause phenomena
and information points in the intonation of the clause. Possible
explanations of this have included Goldman–Eisler's suggestion
(1961) that the longer the pause before a word, the higher the
information value the item carried. For schoolwork, however, the
important issue for the description of language variety is this:
pauses in speech mark out spontaneous colloquial utterances;
where we can invest our written texts with some of the known
features of spontaneous speech features we can make the
written text take on some of the directness and immediacy of
speech – an obvious component in written style. In the opposite
direction, where we can succeed in speaking as if we were reading
from a book, our spoken language can take on some of the formality of types of written language.

It would be completely misleading to suggest that pause
phenomena offer the only marks of speech style in writing.
Unstressed (or reduced) forms of the verb give another good
signal of casual speech styles, *I'm, she'll, he'd've* etc. . . .
Repetitions, broken words and phrases and tongue slips mark

speech forms. Special spellings in written text may be used to recall accent features or dialect pronunciations *gonna, had of, a've,* etc. . . . Occasionally italicisation is used to show the volume or prominence (a combination of volume and stress) of a word in a text and more obviously derived visual metaphors may arise in writing to show speech features, such as smaller or larger letters used to show volume; shaking outlines of letters to suggest (comically) fear or even old age. Since there are few strict conventions governing the use of this last group of 'metaphors' they can occasionally run to graphic fantasy, or into art or humour. Linguistics cannot trace the links between phonic and graphic worlds in these cases, but the notion of *intention* can; when we examine the wider situation of which the text — the cartoon, advertisement, etc. — is part, we can ask quite young native speakers why the writer or artist has written the words like that and we can expect a high proportion of perceptive answers. We have, of course, in our experimental materials, *Discovering Language II*, made classes of thirteen-year-olds familiar with various graphic manipulations, and we have found the critical abilities of these pupils developing rapidly in the field of unconventional writing. In our own view this is a fertile area for school language study, leading easily from class reaction to humorous texts to much deeper considerations of language. Subtle use of graphic forms can lead to sound knowledge of both *mode* and the degree of formality of participation which we call *tenor* for short.

Both *mode* and *tenor* (degree of formality) are terms which look in two directions — back to linguistic phenomena such as clause form, spelling, stress marks, tonality, etc. — and forward into social situation. This illustrates clearly the notion of 'parameter', a term once used fairly freely in 'register' studies. However, it is not the appropriateness or otherwise of this mathematical term 'parameter' which we will deal with here — although we should note that it has caused some confusion in teaching circles — it is the wider issue that our study of language variety is socio-linguistic — we are dealing with relationships within society as much as with relationships within the language system. Consider, for instance, the linguistic items sometimes called *stabilisers* — virtually meaningless items such as *I mean; you know; in fact; well.* These are usually related to that famous term of Malinowski's, *phatic communion,* although there is some cause for worry over the tendency of some linguists to take Malinowski's term to mean any intrusive utterance, which was not his original meaning. A phatic phrase or word has apparent form, but has very low reference meaning weight. But it would be wrong to say it was meaningless. The phrase is chosen by the speaker to perform a function in discourse and that function may be meaningful in different ways. For instance if semantics embraces notions of context and relationships of participants in discourse – both clearly meaningful in a situational sense – then a phrase like 'in fact' or 'well' although not pregnant with meaning in the dictionary sense and although not even significantly part of clause or phrase structure grammatically, although clearly marked in the phonology, must be held to be a meaningful choice of language.

A judge who says, 'There is no basis in fact for the assertion' is using 'in fact' as a material part of the meaning and the form. The phrase is used in dictionary contrast with something like 'in opinion', 'in conjecture', etc., and cognate with 'in reality', 'capable of proof', etc. Formally, the prepositional phrase is used as a clause adjunct. Had the judge said, 'There is no basis, in fact, for the assertion' he has used the phrase as a marker of style, principally. He indicates that he is more casually, more colloquially disposed in his utterance. He has used 'in fact', together with its pauses and phonological 'weakening' to mean something like 'really', 'you know', 'then', etc. If we were to make a distinction between spoken prose and written colloquial speech, we could call the strong use of the phrase 'spoken prose' and the more casual, weaker, use of the phrase 'written speech'.

In fact, a great variety of items fall into the general category of style markers rather than dictionary phrases or words, and many terms cluster round the area labelling these markers: stabilisers, pause fillers, space fillers, empty words and phrases, phatic words and phrases, throw-away items, etc. What we have to realise from the beginning is that in this question we are entering an area of considerable complexity in which an extensive knowledge of phonology will certainly be necessary for a complete analysis, together with a highly sensitive description of contextual meaning. Hesitation phenomena studies have made suggestions about the function of pauses associated with dictionary items (see Goldman–Eisler, 1961, etc.) and with the whole notion of pauses in the clause. Halliday's notion of the *tone group* and its 'information points' is also relevant to a more extensive study of the phatic item in discourse (1966e). A detailed study of this would be beyond the scope of this book, and the needs of teachers, I feel. As teachers we are mainly interested in the capacity native-speaking pupils have to respond to these (and other) style markers. The area may be complex, but the mastery of this kind of item is part of everyday language competence. Thus, a very clear case of the pupil bringing into our classrooms a rich awareness of the functions of his own language may be shown. As teachers, we ought to exploit this effectively in our mother-tongue work on variety of language.

One is reminded again and again in work on style that the art of persuasion appeals to something already half believed by the audience. If this is true of the content of an utterance, it is doubly true of the linguistic features of an utterance. We communicate effectively when we draw on the known, in terms of latent understanding of language in our audience, and on the unknown, in that we add new or 'creative' content to our utterances. One of the tasks of stylistics must be to determine more fully what a native speaker in fact is predisposed to accept in terms of linguistic or stylistic features. A study of hesitation phenomena can rationalise several points of casual colloquial style; recent suggestions on the organisation of message as a feature of the stresses in the tone group (stated as phonology) and as a feature of 'given' and 'new' information in terms of content will almost certainly explain yet more. Linguistics itself contributes to our understanding of the organisation of language, but, more significantly, socio-linguistics links linguistic behaviour with the organisation of society. Clearly, a study of style embraces both, but is more stimulated by socio-linguistic aspects of language in use than by this or that description of language itself. Style is about people.

It is this growing awareness of social issues related to language features that makes one feel that Grierson's Aristotelian approach to rhetoric is being continued by present-day stylistics, particularly the study of style which has arisen as part of the new language programmes for schools, e.g. in the Schools Council material *Language in Use* (1971).[4] Rhetoric, as our teaching forefathers conceived it, is dead, for the very good reason that it was designed for a climate of philosophy and a view of education now no longer of contemporary importance. Each age is marked, as Susan Langer (1949) observed, by its own forms of curiosity, its own modes of enquiry. A socio-linguistic viewpoint is typical of the present-day outlook, and from this, because of the dynamism of linguistic studies, there has emerged the study of rhetoric in a new key.

# NOTES

[1]    The best description of this is to be found in Robins (1951) *Ancient and Mediaeval Grammatical Theory in Europe*. The idea of grammar being at once a philosophy and a method, however, is firmly rooted in school courses.

[2]    In his 1971 paper, *Language in a Social Perspective*, Halliday puts this point. It was largely the point he made in his paper on socio-linguistics at the Cambridge conference of the International Association of Applied Linguistics in September 1969.

[3]    I refer, of course, to M. A. K. Halliday's work, particularly from 1966.

[4]    *Language in Use* is the text for school work produced by the Nuffield, latterly School Council project in Linguistics and English teaching, which ran from 1964–70 in University College, London under the direction of M. A. K. Halliday.

# 8 The Organisation and Grading of Materials

We have implied in the preceding chapters that this study is about the relationship between a body of knowledge and its application to the practical problems of the classroom English syllabus. The body of knowledge is linguistic, psycholinguistic and sociolinguistic and we have already noted that one of the ways in which it affects what we do in English teaching reform is by giving us, as teachers, an orientation to our problems. This orientation extends from the vaguest idea of 'looking in the right direction' to the grading of texts and the selection of methods. This chapter deals with the thinking behind the writing of *Discovering Language II*, the materials produced as an example of a discovery course in English language for average and above average secondary school pupils. The materials discussed here were subjected to school testing in the manner described in Chapter 9, with the conclusions noted at the end of that chapter.

No discussion of the grading of materials could begin without a statement of the aim of our teaching. This has already been made in Chapter 1 but must be made again here. We have taken up the view that English language work in schools shares something of the general aims of education – that an educated man should be able to think rationally and incisively about his environment and the human situation (Gleason, 1964:267). Adapted specifically to the teaching of English language the aim becomes: *that an educated native speaker ought to be able to be rational and articulate about the nature of his mother-tongue and about the relationships which exist between a user of the language and his society.*

The view of the role of the nativeness of the native speaker in our approach is an important one, discussed in some detail in Chapter 5 and elsewhere. He is *homo loquens*; he comes to us speaking his own language, in control, as Palmer says, of subtleties of its grammar and phonology in a way which would be extremely difficult to produce in a foreign speaker of English, even after long and careful teaching. The native speaker has insights to the nature of his language in use. He can, to a greater or lesser degree, manipulate it as a social instrument. He can learn, using its structuring power, psychologically speaking; he has what Halliday has described as 'an intuitive knowledge of what language is and an awareness of the linguistic structuring of experience' (1967d:1). It is intended in the course of teaching the materials discussed below to externalise certain of these native insights and make them part of the educational attainment of the pupil.

Some educationists argue that method and grading cannot be separated (see Mackay, 1965), but this is not our view as we have argued in Chapter 6. Grading is taken to be independent of method. Grading identifies and links the elements of a course; method defines the teacher–pupil–text relationship in abstract terms. A third element implied in the syllabus is teaching technique. We might think of this as the means by which a teacher reaches his pupils in the practical work of instruction, elicitation, etc. which classroom contact demands. It is not a contradiction to say that in the discussion which follows on the grading of the materials, while grading is our principal concern, method and technique will be referred to where it is thought to be useful.

## Overall Sessional Plan

The areas defined in the broad pattern of the course are three:
A.  a study of language *levels*;
B.  an area of more specific study of certain *patterns* of language (surface and deep) associated with form;
C.  a study of *language variety*.

In teaching the materials for the experiment we began with A (levels), worked through B (patterns) and moved on to C (varieties) i.e. A, B, C. Clearly A ought to precede, but there might be, alternatively, a case for looking at C before B, since the contact with the fertile area of varieties of language may be used to sharpen the pupil's awareness of how language patterns play a part in the production of effective texts.

## A Description of the Components of the Course
A.  *Levels*
The theory of language levels, or levels of analysis, is well indicated in European traditional linguistics and in the school courses that have been inspired by traditional linguistics. By

identifying different aspects of utterance or text, e.g. the phonetic or phonological aspect, the grammatical aspect, the semantic aspect, etc. we separate out for study different views of utterance, based on different hypotheses and having different modes of investigation. This helps us to make articulate scientific statements about language and languages; it gives us in effect a heuristic device. Halliday *et al.* in *SHAM* (1964:95, etc.) have referred to the antiquity of the idea of 'aspects' of language, to the usefulness of the concept in linguistics and teaching and to the extensive area of common ground which exists between linguists on this topic (which we have discussed in Chapter 3.2 in our description of Firthian linguistics). A chart showing the similarities of a number of different linguistic systems in the area of levels is given in Mackey (1965:38). It is a very reassuring diagram. The degree of common ground shown is remarkable.

Broadly, the materials of our school course are organised to show that there are at least the following aspects of a language text:
1 its *substance*, that is, the medium in which its information is carried – sound or marks;
2 its *form*, – the more abstract organisation of the text in such areas as syntax, and grammar system;
3 its *meaning*, in which semantic considerations are described.

These areas, *substance*, *form* and *meaning* are linked together by what we might call sub-levels (although I don't want to foist any term other than *link* on to the theory). The link between substance and form is *phonology* (for a spoken text) and *graphology* (for a written text). Clearly, phonology can reflect graphology and *vice versa*, and both kinds of link are exploited in the materials. Finally, *context* is at least one way in which form can relate to the meaning of the language in use.

We are trying in the materials to represent a coherent view of language as a whole. If the idea of a linked set of levels is derived from discussions about the nature and role of language such a 'grid' may act as a kind of map for learners. In the past grammar courses have tended to concentrate on syntax and morphology with related work in semantics. There were few overt references to phonology and the only contact with graphology was through spelling – a piece of course work separated physically and intellectually from grammar in the syllabus. The disregard for substance in school courses – for questions about sounds and writing or printing – has been almost total. It is difficult to think of language work being relevant

115

to mother-tongue speakers without substance being a main part of its matter, having regard to the importance of speech in language use in society.

The pattern of levels we hope to produce in pupils of 13–14 years of age is given below:

**Written** (medium)

Chains
Choices      Meaning
Dictionary

**Spoken** (medium)

If this 'map' of language levels is compared with the diagram of levels given in Chapter 3.2 it will be seen that considerable simplification has been used. The notions of phonic substance and phonology are merged into SPOKEN (medium) and the question of graphic substance and its link with form has been compressed into WRITTEN (medium). Further, the distinction between CHAINS and CHOICES in form indicates a crude distinction between surface grammar and the deep grammar of systems of dependencies, which we shall discuss below. DICTIONARY is a study – not of dictionary meaning, as some might suspect – but of where words fall in relationship to each other in utterances. 'Dictionary meaning' would be one aspect of MEANING.

Spoken and Written Media
It is essential for teachers at many points in their teaching of English language to remind themselves and their classes that language is basically built of physically identifiable sounds, and that these sounds obey the laws of physics like any other sounds. Similarly, in thinking about writing and printed texts with a class, it is useful to go back from time to time to the fundamental idea that writing is a pattern of marks, which behave like any other marks, physically speaking. The first and second lessons of the course cover precisely this aspect of language. Pupils discuss the difficulties of making out space to ground-control two-way radio speech; they talk about distinguishing the words of a hymn sung by a congregation; they discuss mistaken 'words' heard in sounds of animal and bird calls. In brief they use their own experience to establish the principle that in all speech

116

communication the state of the physical signal is of the utmost importance.

In the printed word something similar is done. The class is invited to use its imagination and suggest unusual writing media – patterns of people standing in a field, smoke against the sky, blood, etc. The way advertising can use a medium in which the substance of the marks has a special relevance to the produce being sold can be discussed, e.g. tyre marks to sell tyres. This preliminary discussion brings the idea of substance clearly into focus. Ways in which the substance can be affected, e.g. by distortion, and fading (just like sound) are touched on in class-work, and the question of legibility and typographical appro-priateness is opened up – e.g. can you *read* the signature on a pound note? Finally, the idea of layout contributing to graphic meaning is dealt with; a menu is given as an unpunctuated and un-laid-out text and the class design a menu from the data.

This introduction can lead on to a discussion of the links which exist between substance and form. We can manipulate a word in print to 'look like', say its sound or its meaning. The use of graphic manipulations in teaching – graphic puns if you care for the term – is a fertile and little used device. It is true that it has the force of a gimmick and in the hands of a thoughtless teacher might be used merely as entertainment. But as an explanatory device, with fresh and vital impact, graphic manipulations are buoyant, effective teaching aids. We reproduce the opening panel of examples from lesson 3 below: the first group shows puns on the word meanings; the second puns on the intonational and stress patterns – the sounds – of the words. Pupils discuss the different intentions of the puns and draw their own conclusions, teasing apart notions of phonology from those of semantic meaning.

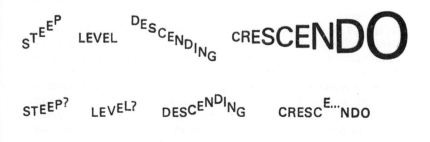

Teachers may have had a similar experience to mine when a film showing the use of graphic manipulations was shown in the cinema recently. It was a film advertising the services of a British bank and words associated with banking like 'interest' were manipulated to illustrate in some symbolic way the notions they represented. The effect on the cinema audience I was part of in Birmingham was striking: there was spontaneous applause. I heard independently from M. A. K. Halliday that a similar reaction to these graphic manipulations had been noticed in London.

Up to this stage, without actually teaching the definition of levels, we have 'discovered' the following points:

**What we see (written)**

| can make us think of | can sometimes look like |
| **what we hear (spoken)** | **what the word means** |

It will be recognised that this is the embryo of the map of levels we discussed earlier in this chapter.

A whole field of practical research can be stimulated in 'puns' dealing with language substance. Television advertising makes wide use of this kind of graphic 'teaching' and it supports it by selected non-language sounds and pictures. My experience of pupil reaction to work in this field is that children welcome assignments out of class and away from class textbooks. Properly handled these assignments can be very fruitful. They exploit predictions the native speaker would make about the appearance and sound of his language in use. This illustrates exactly what we mean when we say that the native speaker is in possession of insights to the nature and use of his own language before we ever teach him about language. The 'discovery' approach to language teaching tries to make use of this knowledge as effectively as possible in its handling of materials. The discovery approach, of course, is much more than the mere appeal to pre-existing knowledge; it involves the highly significant effect on learning which comes from open discussion. Rational discussion, and the 'warming up' talk which precedes it is one of the most important elements in mother-tongue education, and although teachers are often quick to agree with this, one finds very little legislation for open talk in courses or syllabuses.

We have pre-echoed lesson four in the diagram we draw after lesson three. If words can be made to look like their meanings and even to look like their sounds, may they not equally be able to sound like their meanings, or be spelled like their actual sounds? This brings us into the well-trodden area of onomatopoeia and also into the less well-known area of 'sound pictures'. Let me illustrate this: the words *moan* and *croak* seem to be clear attempts to represent an actual sound event in a word at the same time as the word labels an event or a thing. Compare this with a word like *Atishoo*. It represents the sound of the event well, but the label for the event is *sneeze*. A class can be given three lists of words; one is a list of labels only like *explosion, sneeze*; the second list may be of words which both label and represent the sound of the event, like *croak, roar, moan*; the third list can be of words which are graphic sound pictures, like *Atishoo, boo . . . ooommm, ha, ha, ha* and the like. It is a good idea to have pupils study only a few key examples of these three lists and then collect for themselves a list of common examples. Some of the work assignments used with this lesson include writing 'sound pictures' for a rifle shot, the sound of a jazz trumpet, the sound of a rusty hinge opening. Conversely, pupils are invited to give word labels to graphic sound pictures in certain defined contexts, such as *KISSSSHHHH* in the context of the orchestra, and many others.

This would seem to be the ideal time to take our language study into direct contact with literature. What in fact are the onomatopoeic effects in Tennyson's 'The moan of doves in immemorial elms/And murmuring of innumerable bees'; or the cry of the 'ravished nightingale' in Lyly's 'Jug, jug, jug, jug, tereu,'? This is tentatively explored in lesson 4.

These four lessons, plus a review lesson, take us up to an important point in the course. Without in any way exhausting the opportunity the class will have for discussion of graphic and phonic matters in texts, it covers the introduction to such matters. The stage which follows is more abstract, and introduces the notion of form in language.

Form
When we are introducing form as a level of analysis we must try to make our introductory lessons representative of the whole domain. For example, if the eventual model we are likely to use is one in which surface and deep distinctions will be made in grammar, it is necessary to pre-echo this in our earliest lessons.

This suggestion is made in the spirit of Bruner's remark that it is possible to teach any subject to a child at any stage of his development in some intellectually honest way (1960). We thus begin our lessons on form with a lesson on the chain structure of English syntax as a surface phenomenon and after a general discussion of the question of making little flow charts to represent choices in any sphere of activity (choirs, cricket teams, army promotion, etc.), we introduce the idea that language has systems of choice which operate in a similar way. In one sense what we are distinguishing here is the difference between syntagmatic issues and paradigmatic issues. Our view of paradigmatic issues however has considerably advanced since Saussure's proposals (1914), for instance by incorporating systemic proposals associated with Halliday and others, discussed in Chapter 3.2, and we want children to think of choices in the grammar of English being something much more than a table of inflexions such as they might remember from Latin or French teaching; rather, we want pupils to explore through systems the social and morphological resources of English.

There are two related features of syntax which we ought to dwell on here, partly because of their implications for method: the use of 'nonsense' English and the study of poetic and other stylistic inversions of syntactic order. We use both of these in our course. Nonsense English has been in the public mind since Lewis Carroll made it a feature of *Alice in Wonderland*, that remarkably fertile story for children, probably more read by adults than their offspring. '*Twas brillig, and the slithy toves did gyre and gimble in the wabe,*' etc. Of course it can be argued that this 'nonsense' is now accepted as an almost commonplace linguistic event in English. The words have meaning in the context of *Alice in Wonderland*, and, further, they are glossed within the fantasy of the story itself. But the principle of inventing texts which are patently English but which use new lexis is one to which language teachers have been considerably attracted in the last two decades, mainly as a result of structuralism. Paul Roberts uses nonsense sentences to illustrate the nature of structural signals in his *Patterns of English* (1956); Randolph Quirk makes good use of it for similar purposes in *The Use of English* (1962:VII).

Inversions of various kinds in English syntax are well known in school language work. We might almost say they are too well known. One of the grammar books I studied from at school seemed to have the idea that no general analysis was worth its salt unless it were straightening out the contorted sentences of eighteenth-century verse, or other highly stylistically marked texts. Given that there is a usual order for the declarative in English, however, *subject + verb + object*, with the adjunct phrase able to float to several unrestricted positions in the sequence except between verb and object, we can identify syntactic order and deviance effectively. If we have a sentence like 'That wild lion Tom caught' we have ambiguity. It either shows inversion of verb and object, in which case the lion caught Tom, or it shows positioning of the object phrase before subject and verb, in which case Tom caught the lion. When we have established in simple study of chain structure of the clause that there is a 'home' order of elements in places, we can do two things by drawing attention to unusual order of elements. Firstly, we can consolidate the notion of normal order in the declarative clause. Secondly, we can make initial remarks about stylistic re-ordering of syntax. Taking clauses as simple as 'said he', 'retorted the king', 'Bread have I', etc., we can show that where the meaning is not distorted by the inversion, a 'poetic' or 'rhetorical' effect can be achieved by inversion. This is done minimally in Lesson 6.

The choice of words is dealt with in two lessons in the materials used, Lessons 8 and 9. In the first, the question of classification of words as grammatical items is contrasted with the selection of words for appropriate meaning. In the second, the idea of words being linked in utterances by collocational affinities is dealt with. The classification of a word as a grammatical item merely means to a pupil at this stage, that the right kind of word has been chosen for the phrase. It is fairly easy for a pupil to establish that a speaker saying, 'He drives the . . . em . . . excavator', paused while the search for the right kind of word with the right meaning was undertaken. Had the utterance been 'He drives the . . . em . . . thingumybob', it would be clear that while the grammatical requirements of the clause had still been satisfied – a noun had been signalled by 'the . . .' and had eventually appeared. Naturally a noun may be full of meaning, in the dictionary sense, or more or less empty of meaning. Normal conversation uses many items of the correct grammatical class, but for numerous reasons, of low semantic weight. 'The thing on the car in front is blinking.' Pupils have their own examples, some of them collectors' items.

Lexis
There are certain areas of language use where a teacher may feel

intuitively that there is considerable value in study, but where linguistic theory has not a great deal to offer. It would be uncharitable to say that in the study of lexis linguistics had been idle. Far from it; a considerable amount of ingenuity and thought has been invested in lexical study in recent years and work continues. Yet, linguists are not entirely happy about the preliminary statements on lexis which these recent studies have produced. Teachers, however, have used and are still using the notions of *collocation* and *set* tentatively suggested by linguists and they report much to support the approach in classroom work.

Basically, the theory suggests that since all lexical items are not equally likely in a given place in structure, restrictions of collocation (sequential co-occurrence of words) and set (group of words restricted by subject) should be explored. It would not be unlikely to find 'waves' and 'sea' closely linked in a text sequence. 'Waves of scrap iron' would transmit to us a kind of lexical shock – albeit an agreeable one, since the metaphor might be effective. Operating from the notion of predictability of words falling together in utterances or texts, we can, at once, approach the question of mutual linkage of words in text and, in an unambitious way rationalise something of the lexical choices of language. If you like, we are looking again at the notion of a thesaurus, but on the one hand it is linked with syntax and on the other, style. Lesson 9 covers this idea.

Context
Semantics has for long been the area of linguistic interest most exploited by schools. Word and phrase meanings are always studied in comprehension; changes in meaning of words are noted; dictionaries are issued to classes and various 'dictionary exercises' are undertaken. In brief, the broadly defined area of word meaning is recognised as a vital one for school language study. In our materials we have specifically dwelt on context as an important aspect of meaning. If all language is part of a wider human situation, we can say that what a word or phrase, etc., means will depend largely on what the context of utterance is. Firth writes interestingly about this (1964:X) by asking 'What do the words mean?' and answering it apparently circularly 'They mean what they do.' He takes the utterance 'Say when' and explores its meaning. He speaks of the furniture of the room in which the remark was made, its occupants, their behaviour, the casual friendly feelings – glasses (or tea cups) being filled up.

The meaning of 'say when' is defined by its context. Had the context not been that of social entertaining, but had involved someone with his mouth wide open, a doctor with a spatula pressed down on the root of the tongue, the feelings of slight discomfort, a tendency to retch, and anxiety, the doctor's request 'say when' would have borne a vastly different meaning from the first example.

One of the most useful ways of using the notion of context in work with pupils is to give the class an uncontextualised phrase or clause and ask them to fill in the context and thus delimit the meaning. Alternatively, the class can be given a phrase which could be ambiguous until contextualised and they could explain both meanings. 'A vessel full of oil . . .' (sailing up the Thames) ; 'It's in the net . . .' (and it's a whopper). The identity of the person making the remark or using the phrases, words, etc., often colours the meaning we allocate to the language — i.e. speaker recognition is part of context. Thus, a banker and an architect might both talk about *small change*; pupils can give fuller contexts and meanings. A holidaymaker, a soldier and a gangster might all use the term *the front*; what would it mean in each context ?

Many jokes common in school depend on double contexts. 'The cure for water on the brain is a tap on the head.' There is, of course, a pun involved, a typical grisly schoolboy attitude to disease and the element of the ridiculous. But context defines all this. Classes will make up their own jokes once the idea of context begins to be understood. One school I dealt with (one of the seven experimental schools) produced a sheet of jokes stimulated by this lesson, some of which showed an acute sense of context.

Riddles operate on the principle that parts of the context, often heavily disguised, are given to the hearer and he is asked to guess the name of the thing. We use riddles in Lesson 10 with the other work on context. There would seem to be a good opportunity at a point like this for linking our language work with literature. Good collections of prose and verse riddles exist, some translated from old English, some in collections of eighteenth- and nineteenth-century nursery rhyme books. In the poems of William Soutar a wide range of riddles in Scots and in English will be found. Language study essentially leads out of a closer study of texts to wider reading like this, and the best English teacher, to my mind, will make the most of a point of interest raised, such as context of situation.

123

### B. *Patterns*

The initial contact with patterns of chain and choice, described in Section A (Lessons 6 and 7) may be taken as having paved the way for a closer look at some patterns in English. In an English course for thirteen-year-olds what are these patterns to be and how closely ought we to study them? I have taken my cue in selecting the noun phrase as the starting point of pattern study from two things. Firstly, the frequency of noun phrases in clause structure in English is very high; secondly, the noun phrase, properly studied, can lead on to almost every other aspect of form, and, we might add, to many of the features of style in English.

The functional notion of the noun phrase labelling things is a good starting point. Suppose we had a map – a non-language event, save for minimal naming of rivers, towns, lakes, etc. The features of the terrain indicated by the map give us a number of things which may be labelled by one word – *mountain, bay, road, bridge,* etc. That is, we can construct a number of single word labels. Arguing that these single word labels are not precise enough for a purpose like describing where we fished or swam or stayed on holiday, we can introduce the idea of constructing larger labels on the pattern Pre-headwords + Headwords. We can make up *the northern village; the mountain road; the island castle.* If we want to we can fill the pre-head place with several suitable words, *the small northern seaside village,* etc.

What we have done so far, in about ten minutes of class time at the most, is to point to one feature of the surface structure of the noun phrase, that it has a headword and may have pre-head elements which functionally define more closely the reference of the headword. At this stage in the lesson it is useful to open up class discussions on the notion that there are many more applications of pre-head elements like *northern, seaside, mountainous, lakeside,* etc., than there are of typical headwords like *mountain, sea, lake, river,* etc. Further, with a good class of thirteen-year-olds, one can take a class example with four or five elements in the pre-head place in the noun phrase, say, *the six northern lakeside cottages* and by open discussion, get the class to suggest that there is a declining element of generality from the left to the right in the phrase – the left hand elements tend to define and limit the element next on the right.

In classwork, to try to break away from the traditional form of grammar exercises, we tried several things, one of which was drawing seven triangles each with a different finish, e.g. hatched with close vertical lines, pepper-and-salt spotted and the like. The pupils tried, using the formula pre-head + head, to give resourceful descriptions of what they saw in each. In actual class handling, this exercise produced some highly imaginative noun phrases of the right structure. (Lesson 13)

Why bother to give thirteen-year-olds a vocabulary of description, such as the noun phrase analysis we have outlined? The answer to this is probably best given from language use, although there is a perfectly reasonable argument that any kind of analysis relevant to the children's own use of language is intellectually valuable. Taking the notion of language in use, how can we show that outside the schoolroom – away from the fashioned exercise – the noun phrase is something we would like to talk about. In Lesson 14 we look carefully at James Stephens' poem *The Main-Deep*. We print it below:

THE MAIN-DEEP

The long-rolling,
Steady pouring,
Deep-trenchèd
Green billow:

The wide-toppèd
Unbroken,
Green-glacèd
Slow-sliding

Cold-flushing,
– on – on – on –
Chill-rushing,
Hush-hushing,
. . . Hush-hushing . . .

Pupils begin by talking about waves, and what they look like breaking, what they sound like, and when a wave is 'over' and when it is not. Then they look at the structure of the poem, linguistically. What is the headword of the first stanza – *billow*. Does it end the noun phrase there? Why does ending the noun phrase there give us a double kind of satisfaction – language pattern and wave description? What is the structure of the second 'wave'; how many stanzas does this unbroken wave flow over;

125

does the language reflect this ? These questions and all the other interesting ones which the class themselves ask and prompt, form the basis of a discovery process in which what we know about the structure of language, a simple thing in this case about the NP, contributes towards our being able to say something more about the effect of the poem. We may not actually assert that the poet calculated with his noun phrases before writing the actual stanzas. Quite the reverse; we have used a little bit of linguistic knowledge to get a handhold on meaning in the poem. What we have done is after the fact of the poem's creation.

The noun phrase in its fuller form *pre-head* + *head* + *post-head* opens up the notion of embedding (minimally) with this stage of study. The post head elements of a noun phrase are usually in the form of a prepositional phrase like *in the city* or a possessive in prepositional form *of the north*; the interesting thing is that, although we might have considerable difficulty in determining the precise semantic function of such embedded phrases, we can happily allocate them to a place in structure. We are conscious of the difference at a deep level between *A Book of Birds* and *Children of the Wind* (both book titles – a useful source of interesting labels) but we can perform at least surface bracketing of the elements without necessarily involving ourselves or our classes in the deeper semantic issues involved.

Embedding, or rankshifting, means that a phrase is used as part of another phrase, whereas we might expect the hierarchically orthodox situation to be that a phrase entered into the structure of a clause. But we can show clauses entering into noun phrase structure. While we do not necessarily want to go into this at this stage in the school, unless there were good reason for it, like talking about a text in which a defining as opposed to a non-defining adjective clause was used for a certain effect, we can see that noun phrases by their resourcefulness in embedding other phrases and clauses, and by themselves being embedded, involved in clause structure at subject, object and adjunct place, offer almost a round tour of surface (and some not so surface) syntax. Nouns, noun phrases and the idea of nominality should be one of the fundamental areas of linguistic enquiry on which we draw in teaching. The socio-linguistic and stylistic implications of nouns and their compounds are well discussed in *Grammar, Society and the Noun* (Halliday, 1967) and a wide range of interesting school applications might be stimulated by some of the examples given. Halliday's remark in this booklet 'We grow up in a nominalized environment' might well be the guiding principle of a whole course of syntax, highly relevant to the everyday use of language.

It is by no means the object of this course to produce for the schools merely another form of general analysis to replace a dying and even already dead one. The key word of our work is that the pupils should be rational and articulate about language in use. In our view knowledge of how language works may be a vital element in the structuring of learning; at a more mundane level, knowledge of how language patterns can be a critical tool of known socio-linguistic and stylistic worth. In clause analysis we try to handle only these main ideas: (i) the notion of *process* (Lesson 14) and (ii) the concept of the *clause chain* (Lessons 14 and 15). The first of these is a concept of the deep organisation of the clause. For example identification of process may lead on to questions of actor and goal; questions of extensive and intensive action and ascription, which would reveal three important features of transitivity. At this stage, however, we allow the class merely to turn the notion of process over in their minds when they are faced with ambiguity, *can* as either noun or verb in *can fish*; *giant waves*; *American cranes*, etc. A certain amount of joking, like this, can be salutary. Class research can help by throwing the net wide and bringing in newspaper headlines, telegrams or advertisement copy where the notion of *process* and of *'thingness'* can be seen to be distinguished in different uses of the same word, or in ambiguous texts. Tense is an aspect of process on which mood can be shown to be dependent. My own aim with the second form Scottish classes we taught in the experiment was to focus on the idea of process and mention tense in passing.

The clause chains we presented were simple ones – *a name label + a process + a thing label*. To many this will seem unambitious, but when it is seen as a starting point for thinking about nominality and the role of subject, process and the notion of transitivity and goal, also in terms of transitivity, it can be seen that all we need at this stage in syntax is a framework of an open nature. A certain amount of practice in chain manipulation is advisable, and both Lessons 15 and 16 provide this. Diaries are rewritten in full clauses, pupils are asked to talk about a railway timetable and then to say why they constructed their clauses as they did. Simple logical exposition and the use of appropriate clause chains and tenses are closely linked. Traditionally the synthesis exercise, the paragraph rewritten from jumbled events and similar work tested skills in this area. Our intention has been to take a fresh look at this area of language and as far as seemed useful at this stage, to rationalise something of what we discovered in language in use. Above all, we are trying to produce in pupils an awareness of patterning in language which is not a school dead end subject, but which can lead on to wider and more delicate rationalisations about language form of use in social questions and in style.

## C. *Language Variety*

In Chapter 7 we have explored at some length the revived interest in language varieties, which we characterise broadly by the term 'rhetoric'. This third section of the materials presents a classroom approach to language variety which embraces aspects of what teachers have called 'register studies', or, sometimes, 'styles', 'varieties' and in a few cases 'rhetoric'. In short, this is a critical study of texts – both written and spoken. It is an attempt to bring into focus some of the richness of English in present-day use. In a very practical sense this sector of a mother-tongue language course attempts to help pupils to gain a handhold on an aspect of language in use which is intuitively recognised by native speakers as a vital, dynamic and often exciting part of normal life.

A study of varieties inevitably involves the two-way relationship which exists between written and spoken texts. A spoken text, such as conversation or discussion, may be written down in a number of ways. The particular way it is written is a great source of class interest. Do we try to represent *all* of the heard text – the noises of the pronunciation features, the slips of the tongue, etc. – or do we select only some of these? In fact, all transcriptions – phonetic and orthographic – do compromise between full phonic recording, economy and selection. A single message however might be studied *a.* in its fully written form, *b.* in its written-to-look-like-spoken form – say within the conventions of written dialogue – or *c.* in some kind of orthographic imitation (transcription) of the spoken form. Discussion of the different realisations follows and some of the features of special styles and writing styles are shown. In this work, as in most 'discovery' teaching, the technique is one of *reaction* to and *discussion* of the contrasts involved in the text. *Tout revient à la différence.*

The section on varieties with experimental materials opens with two lessons dealing with the similarities and differences between spoken and written language in use. For example we

128

present a lesson with a single message in writing which successively shows how the message might have been encoded as we describe in the preceding paragraph. If we tried to write down *exactly* what we thought we heard over the telephone, or if we used conventions of written dialogue, say, for a novel or short story, what would the encoding of the message look like? If we made a written report of our telephone conversation, what would the language be?

From this encounter with differences in style relating to whether a text is nearer representation of speech or nearer the style(s) of writing we can ask a class to think broadly in terms of 'more' or 'less' representation of spontaneous speech in the text being studied. The written word can be modified in many ways to show spoken features. Some of these modifications are accepted within the conventions of English spelling, like the reduced forms of the verbs *I'm, we're, sh'd've, he'd've* and of the negative marker, *hadn't, couldn't*. Other tricks of writing attempting to convey characteristics of spoken language in written texts are unconventional in the strictest sense – that is, there is no formal convention embracing the modifications. Examples of unconventional modifications might include dots to indicate pause phenomena, dashes and other special graphic features like letter size, italicisation, degree of inking and in some texts use of colour.

Although we speak of this as a new area for school exploration, in a way this is misleading. Teachers have always recognised the existence of modified texts showing colloquial forms. Usually, teachers have either identified these as curiosities, or have condemned them as errors. It is our view that idiosyncrasies of text are often highly successful in underlining characteristics of the language in use. Further, work in the field of language varieties in a broad sense leads pupils to range widely over effective use of language in a much wider area of text than schools have in the past allowed. The Victorian notion that speech was subordinate to writing, because writing was permanent and speech was transitory, was wrong in theory, but further, can be shown no longer to apply in any practical sense, since we have for some decades now been recording the living speech of native speakers. What would have made our forefathers shudder, in terms of slips of the tongue, repetitions, broken patterns and hesitations, are now seen to be part of an elaborate marking system of colloquial or spontaneous speech. Where this system affects writing directly, a degree of freshness and realism may be produced, and many modern novels, modern advertising copy and types of journalism make extensive use of the fertile contact which can result from spoken and written styles.

In our materials we explored several different types of written text — a strip cartoon story, a play and a short series of extracts from books — to exemplify the spoken — written links further. Practical research for the class in both chapters dealt with careful listening to actual conversation (what do we hear; what do we leave in and what do we leave out?) and we stimulated careful critical study of advertising and its use of the colloquial signals.

A native-speaking child builds up a wide experience of his language world. Even quite young children will recognise a wide assortment of styles. A child might say 'That's like my school reader'. 'That's from a comic!' 'Our school notice board has messages like that', etc., etc., and it is a very valuable piece of class language work to discuss the source of a text. If we make these texts very varied, as in lesson 20 (below), we can tap a wide variety of texts. *Source* is a socio-linguistic feature of style. The child with wide reading and observation will naturally do outstandingly well, but even the less able teenager can sparkle in class when he is dealing with source identification. A 'bookish' boy may not have the width of experience of advertising graphics that his lively but unacademic neighbour may have. One of the great values of source-and-subject discussions in class is that for the right answer to be given (or a careful deduction of where a text might have appeared) a whole range of internalised responses to language must be made. Of course people remember styles and can identify them sometimes by quite trivial features; but it is much more usual for pupils to talk their way towards an answer on source. What is the passage about? Are there any special graphic features? What kind of reader do you imagine was aimed at? Who might write like this? What effects or intentions did he have in mind? Questions like this do not merely explore the form of a given text; they plumb the spectrum of socio-linguistic existence. In terms of practical classwork, such discussions often result in the liveliest and most rewarding explorations of text imaginable, with side-issues and touchstones by the score.

As an illustration of such a lesson, I print an example below. It deals with *source* and *style* and leads on to *parody*. It was in fact Lesson 20 of the experimental materials.

## LESSON 20
## NOW, WHERE WAS THAT WRITTEN?

When you see a piece of written English for the first time, you can often make a good guess at where it might have been quoted from. The *source* of a piece of writing is quite often indicated by clues in the passage itself. Sometimes these clues are in the way the text is printed and set down; sometimes the clues are in the way the language is organised; sometimes the clues are in the way words are chosen. Often all these things, and your own experience, work together to tell you the source of a quoted text.

We are often far more expert than we think in working out where a text might have appeared. Let's try a few.

a. SLEEVES
Using No. 11 needles, cast on 36 sts.
Work in K.1, P.1 rib for $2\frac{1}{4}$ins.

b. 'Stand!' cried Alan, and pointed his sword at him.
The Captain stood, indeed; but he neither winced nor drew back a foot.
'A naked sword?' says he. 'This is a strange return for hospitality.'

c. I staggered ashore with my nine fish weighing just over twenty-seven pounds in all. The fishing had taken one hour, and it remains in my mind as perhaps the finest hour of my fishing career.

## DISCUSSION
1   The way the texts are laid out and printed helps us to place two of these passages. Discuss this, pointing out the features of the appearance of the texts concerned.
2   One of the texts given is clearly a little bit old-fashioned in its use of language. Which? Just say what seems to you to be old-fashioned. You needn't go deeply into the question.
3   Each text has a special vocabulary. List the main words briefly and say whether they help you to be sure of *what* was being dealt with in the text concerned and *where* such a text might have appeared.

131

4   Talk together about unusual pieces of writing you have
    seen. Perhaps someone has seen the Lord's Prayer etched
    on a silver threepenny piece, or someone may have seen the
    instructions given on the controls inside an astronaut's
    space capsule.

WORK
1   Sometimes the way a text is written down gives you a very
    good clue to where you would find a similar piece of
    language in use. Here are several passages which you should
    examine carefully. Write notes on the features of the
    appearance of the text that helped you in deciding the source
    of each. Give the source you thought of.

a.

b.  The pi-per came to our town, To our ... town, to our
    ... town, The pi-per came to our town, And he play'd
    bon-nie-lie

c.  HIGHGATE: s/c flatlet. c.h.w., 4 gns plus baby-sitting.
    ABB 6499

2   These passages (below) *may* have appearances which help
    you to tell where they might have been used, but it is more
    likely that you will find the clues you seek in the patterns
    and words used in the texts. Look over the passages care-
    fully and write down a source and a use for each. Then try
    to explain in a note what features of the language (patterns
    or words) helped you most in coming to a decision.
a.  US buyer found for Queen Mary

b.  CASTLE COMBE – (Rail to Chippenham, then by bus)
    Countless photographs have been taken of the ancient
    three-arched bridge, backed by the picturesque house of

Castle Combe, for it is one of the most enchanting villages of Wiltshire.

c.  There was once a little sparrow

**3**  It is possible to find a passage that *looks* as if it should deal with subject 'A', but in fact, on reading it carefully, one finds it deals with quite another subject in the *style* we would expect to be typical of 'A'. This is called *parody*, and it can be used to give a humorous effect. Naturally, when we are guessing the source of texts, we have to know whether the author was intentionally writing one text in the style of another.

For example, here is one man's description of an army:

'Take ten thousand discontented men, one thousand over-bearing aristocrats determined to be leaders, and dress all in uncomfortable clothes. Mix the men thoroughly and allow to stand for several years cooling off, then agitate under the conditions of war.'

This bitter comment on the army is in the form of a cooking recipe.

Try a parody of your own, not necessarily a bitter comment, of course. Think of a clearly marked style, perhaps one of the styles we have used in this Chapter, and use it for an unusual purpose. If you can think of nothing, try writing some of the rules of the Highway Code in the fashion of a very religious sermon.

RESEARCH
Look during the week at the captions (texts) below pictures. Note any special features that arise in the language because it is used with 'visual aids'.

Where tape recordings of conversation, or other styles of spoken language are available (or make them yourself) a further dimension of source study can be promoted. Accent features, often only vaguely hinted at in written texts, are best treated in this way. I have seen a class erupt with ideas over accent. True, many of the ideas were prejudice: *He thinks he's better than us. His father's probably some great man, or something.* Both of these responses were produced by playing a tape to an Edinburgh school class of a northern English grammar school class discussion of poetry. The accents were misinterpreted and being exposed to their unfamiliarity, even some of the more articulate Scottish pupils felt insecure. The discussion which followed on accents, was, to my mind, a very valuable contribution to liberal education.

What we described as the *tenor* of discourse in Chapter 6 dealt with the familiar notion that language sets up a relationship between its participants. Both spoken and written texts can be studied from this point of view. In lesson 21 we looked into the different consequences resulting from 'no parking' signs being composed in different ways. The rather chummy 'Sorry! No parking here' was contrasted with signs running to the stiff 'Motorists are reminded that it is ILLEGAL for unauthorised persons to PARK their CARS within hospital precincts'. Pupils were invited to collect examples of their own, and to compose examples of all kinds of public texts varying from the jocular reminder to the legalistic caveat. The course suggested some work in this area, but classes brought fresh and locally impressive examples into each lesson. This is, of course, the essence of the search-and-discover approach we are adopting.

Two slightly more traditional areas of style take up later lessons (22 and 23). In the first place we looked briefly at the nature of persuasion. This is again a socio-linguistic field. How do you appeal to people when you want them to buy your washing machine? What effect on an uneducated reader does pseudo-scientific jargon have? How can we make a reader react with confidence to a selling suggestion we make, etc.? These questions involve not only content, but form. Lesson 22 takes the opportunity of identifying statement, question, command (or exhortation) and label as four formally different approaches to 'selling' the same message.

Secondly, we explored the basis of parody in Lesson 23. If we can make a good guess at source and intention of a given extract, using our mother-tongue experience, can we detect cases where a style normally associated with a given subject and intention is used purposely with another set of subject and intention? This is an important stylistic issue, drawing on latent knowledge of the language as well as insight to language in use in the community.

LESSON 23
IMITATING STYLES

Most of us would recognise text a. as a Will

a. I, MRS. MARY SMITH, Widow, residing at One Hundred Alma Road, Lennox, do hereby Dispone and Bequeath to my two grandsons, John Dow and James Dow share and share alike and the survivor of them, my whole means and estate.

A label attached to a Christmas present could read:
b. I, ROBERT JOHN JONES, Husband, residing at Ten Oak Road do hereby Give and Donate to my wife, Janet Joyce Jones this gold watch, face and case, hands and dial to be enjoyed by her as a timepiece or portable clock.

## DISCUSSION
1 Text b. is clearly meant to be a joke. Why is it funny? Giving a present is not in itself a joke.
2 How does the language of the Christmas present label make you think of the language of the will? In your discussion you might want to think about the use of capital letters, unusual words, pairs of words and care in the expression.
3 Can you think of another 'joke' way of labelling a gift?

## WORK
1 a. Write down instructions for boiling an egg.
  b. Now write the same instructions in the style you would use if you were writing rules for a game, like Ludo.

Here follow more exercises and a Research topic.

In class, parodies give a bright and often funny and memorable lesson. They also face pupils with some of the most difficult pieces of practical composition the course asks for. In my own teaching of parody I found that even the best classes could show themselves adept at recognising parodies, and talking intelligently about them, but found the production of parodies of a similar sort very difficult indeed. The course was not designed as a composition study, however, and although class teachers, finding this interesting disparity between recognition and production might want to work on the productive side to develop it, during the experiment, I was unable to do this. I had to content myself with encouraging the regular class teacher to follow it up.

The section of the materials on language varieties finished with a summary of the approach to different styles and a review of work which revised the whole section (Lessons 24 and 25).

In the course of the 25 lessons we tried to develop what we believe to be a latent native awareness of language in use and to externalise this as a subject of rational discussion. The description of language which is used in this (and is fed in at points where the principle has been revealed in open discussion) is far less important than the process of discovery. The scheme of each lesson — talk, work, research — is a very important one, however, and is the basis of the creative approach we believe the course typifies.

It is very important that the materials themselves, discussed above, are seen as one teacher's approach to the discovery method of teaching English. In the experimental teaching, I was at once a director of operations generally, and a practical teacher, taking charge of two of the classes involved. I found the lessons buoyant and stimulating to handle, but that testimony might be thought worthless since I wrote the course. I was very encouraged by the reports I had from the teachers who collaborated, and even if we allow for the 'innovation effect' — sometimes called the 'Hawthorn effect' — which teachers and experimental subjects experience during an experiment, I think we can claim that the course was satisfying in the practical work of the English class.

# 9 The School Testing of the Materials

Two principles underlie the argument of this book; firstly, that reform of the English syllabus should arise from the practical needs of the classroom; secondly, that innovations should be scrutinised and tested in the most rigorous and effective way. The thinking of this book has led to a set of materials, representative of a new development in language teaching for native speakers. The materials themselves, later published as *Discovering Language II*, were written in the light of historical, linguistic and practical classroom attitudes; together with the less precise notion 'experience of English teaching' these approaches have directed the methods and handling of the course. Essentially, however, the materials remain one teacher's approach to the teaching of language to English-speaking pupils. The problem of testing the course thus raised a number of issues which, one believes, other teachers must also face when they try to gauge the effectiveness of courses they have designed and taught.

The basic purpose of testing is to measure in quantifiable terms the performance of individuals or groups in the attainment of a specific learning goal. An ideal assessment would include the following characteristics: *a.* that the content of the test or tests would be representative of every aspect of the domain in which achievement is to be assessed; *b.* that the evaluation should yield an ordered series of scores valid in respect of some acceptable criterion and statistically relatable, score to score, as a true basis of comparison (Pilliner, 1968). Clearly, practical limitations exist for test construction. No domain can be totally represented, and time for testing is short. Therefore, a test must make a principled selection of relevant matter from the area to be tested. In selection, however, the domain must be adequately mapped. In this selection, two very important issues must be discussed: one, what is the relationship between the test and the experimental materials; two, what is the role of linguistic theory in mapping the domain?

Wiseman (1961) has categorised tests into *a.* syllabus specific tests and *b.* achievement or goal-specific tests. The former sample and measure what has been taught. That is, they are directly representative of and geared to the syllabus. The latter, goal-specific tests, measure the degree of attainment of the educational objectives proposed. The goal set for the teaching of our experimental materials was that native-speaking children might, in part at least, be able to be rational and articulate about the relationships which exist between a user of language and his society. In terms of measurable achievement, this implies that a native speaker becomes more aware of the linguistic contrasts within utterances and texts and becomes more able to externalise the intuitive and experiential responses to these contrasts which are the mark of a normal user of the language. We have argued that the normal native speaker is defined as a user of the mother-tongue who possesses these insights to the structure and use of his language necessary for proper socio-linguistic adjustment to his society. Thus in our population we are hypothesising a body of insight and in our course we attempt to make it external, rational and manipulable knowledge.

Let us assume that a test T attempts to measure native speaker awareness of the nature and social function of the native language. The course DL attempts to develop a rational awareness of English in use. The syllabus — seen here as the content of the course — is merely a means to an end — a way in which the specified aims of language education are to be achieved. In Wiseman's words, we hold that the test 'Evaluates learning — and teaching — in terms of the aims of the curriculum, and so fosters critical awareness, good method and functional content' (1961 : 6).

Linguistic theory is a necessary instrument in specifying the aim in detailed terms, and in analysing and clarifying the goal. Linguistics is a descriptive instrument in parallel with the language. It is not by any means the only parallel instrument, but for the purposes of this study is the most important one. It maps out the domain; without linguistic theory of some sort no description could be made of language other than in terms of broad social or cultural phenomena. Linguistic theory lies behind part of the process of grading the materials, behind part of the method of teaching the materials and behind the rationale of testing. We would emphasise, however, that we are not teaching linguistic theory; nor are we testing it.

The shape of the experiment might be summarised thus. We have specified and made concrete (as far as possible) a teaching goal in terms of terminal behaviour. We have devised a test which explores the insights to language which exist in the population tested. We have taught the materials DL to a representative population of pupils and we have related improvements in scores in the test to the performance of control groups of pupils attempting to achieve the goal by other means. It is thus possible to claim that by setting up objectives and showing by testing that DL has been successful in some measure in achieving them, we have implied content validity of both the teaching and the testing programme. This allows us to make at least the weak claim that the approach we have used – relying on linguistics, psycholinguistics and socio-linguistics – has been relevant to the practical needs of mother-tongue learning in the schools.

The test T (see Appendix A) was a multiple choice instrument focusing on the recognition of two main areas of linguistic contrast, the concepts implicit in distinctions between levels of analysis (see Chapter 3.2), and the concepts implicit in distinctions of language variety. Two other areas of linguistic awareness are represented in the test – comprehension of a written text and reaction to what would be popularly called 'error' in texts. The text of test T is given in the appendix.

Some remarks on the construction and handling of the test may be relevant. Both taped and written cues were used and in this way listening comprehension as well as reading skills were involved. While it could be argued that semantic skills were involved throughout, in that all frames had to be interpreted, certain specific areas of semantic skill were tested, for example in finding out whether pupils could select different meanings for the same item, e.g. 'a hand'. Areas of grammatical response were tested in two ways. Firstly, an 'odd man out' technique was employed. An item different in its grammatical structure (but perhaps not necessarily different in meaning) was to be selected from a family of patterns three of which were of a kind. Secondly, a pattern was given and the pupil had to select from a group another pattern most like it in its structure.

For practical reasons the test had to be restricted to one class hour. Pupils finished the paper in about 45 minutes and handling time accounted for the remaining fifteen minutes. While no claims are made that the test exhaustively explored the areas on question, it is held that it was representative of the domain dealt with by the course.

The selection of a population and its division into experimental and control groups yielded the following pattern. The experimental course was designed for the second year of the Scottish senior secondary school (grammar school) or for the beginning of the second stage of English study in a comprehensive, i.e. after the common course or introductory stage of English study. We believe that the course used effectively represents the first academic stage of English study in the secondary school.

Seven selected schools took part in the experiment involving 381 pupils as experimental subjects and 197 pupils as controls. Two schools were located in Edinburgh, two in Glasgow, one was east of Scotland rural, one west of Scotland rural and the seventh was a large secondary school in Aberdeen. A cross-section of the social and regional distribution of Scottish senior secondary pupils was reflected in this choice.

The pupils tested were all of average ability and above (they were grammar school pupils). The lowest I.Q. was 92 and the highest 140+. The mean I.Q. of the experimental classes was 118·4 and of the control classes 116·2. The age range was 13·5 to 14·5 years. The control system was based on class similarity. Schools were chosen for the experiment which had identical or very similar second-year classes undertaking language work for similar school goals. Thus in our seven schools, where seven separate heads of English had settled on English language courses of a non-innovatory 'traditional' sort, we were able to take over a suitable second-year class, provide it with our own course to be handled by the ordinary class teacher and while the controls completed their ordinary course in English language the experimental classes followed the special course taking one class hour only in each week – the hour normally set aside for language work in the schools concerned. During the course of the experiment the materials were kept in school and issued only for class lessons to the experimental group. Thus no contamination of the control groups took place.

In terms of continuity the materials were designed to be used for one school period in each week throughout the school session, except for the usual losses through examinations, school functions, holidays and other normal contingencies. All schools finished the course. Test T was set initially and finally to all groups, both experimental and control. An I.Q. test preceded the initial test. No other tests were necessary since the population was taken as representative of a cross-section of the senior secondary school, intellectually, socially, regionally and denominationally. Further, a pooling of scores in the statistical analysis eliminated any stray local variable and I.Q. was specially dealt with by an analysis of co-variance, described below.

The statistical treatment of the scores began with an analysis of gains in test T. This was done by an analysis of variance. This statistical procedure is an analysis of a particular test score in the light of other measured test variables in a given population. It is a particularly useful and elegant treatment of quantities when it has been found that it is impossible to hold a range of test variables constant to leave only one free variable for analysis (e.g. by matching). The technique allows simultaneous consideration of several factors, such as group by group or school by school comparisons in the test.

The sources of 'variance' used in our experiment were obviously the scores achieved in test T before and after the teaching of the materials. That is, on initial testing of the whole population (experimental and controls) there were differences in scores noted between groups and between schools. The significance of these differences was assessed statistically. The performance of the groups within individual schools was studied and finally the pooled results of all experimental groups *vis à vis* all control groups over all schools was calculated. In this way we were able to eliminate random idiosyncracies of a given class (proportion of girls, presence of the children of school teachers, etc.). Further, single classes with only, say, thirty pupils in each were too small to give variance. Within given schools, only two of the seven individually showed significant gains of experimental classes over controls, but when the scores were pooled, there was a highly significant result on the second performance in test T in favour of the experimental subjects (Sig at 1%).

The analysis of co-variance which was carried out on the scores was to test for the relationship between the I.Q.'s of the pupils tested and the scores in test T. Thus we were in fact answering the question 'In how far can we account for the differences in final performance in test T in terms of the differences in I.Q. noted?' In this calculation again, the pooled scores showed that there was a highly significant result confirming that, overall, I.Q. could not be held to account for the improvement of scores of the language test T. Here again it should be noted that individual school class populations are statistically too small for satisfactory projections using co-variance.

We have not published all our statistics here, partly because they might be thought less important for teachers than the results. Further, this kind of testing and its treatment is somewhat specialised and this book is designed for a body of teachers. We should perhaps note that the testing model for this experiment was designed under the guidance of the Godfrey Thomson Unit for Educational Research, of Edinburgh University, and with the help of a grant from my college (Jordanhill College of Education, Glasgow) the statistics were computed by machine under the supervision of Dr. A. E. Pilliner of the Research Unit. I am very much indebted to the Unit for their guidance on these matters, and to the Governors of my college for their help in making such a full statistical treatment of the results possible.

The conclusions we can draw from the testing are these. We have used goal-specific testing approaches in which we have made our educational aim explicit and have established by initial testing that the population was possessed of certain insights to the nature of the mother-tongue in use (as defined by the test). We have subjected a typical school population to experimental teaching and control, and have established that a gain in the insights tested by us may be distinguished for the experimental subjects; this gain is significantly greater for experimental pupils than controls. To eliminate the major variable of I.Q. we carried out an analysis of co-variance and the results show conclusively that I.Q. cannot be held to account for the gains noted in our experimental groups. Pooled scores in both treatment of gains and in the analysis of co-variance eliminate random minor variables not already eliminated by the choice of the representative population.

In broad terms we believe that the materials of the experimental course, and their handling, produced the increased awareness of language in use which we aimed for at the beginning of the experiment. We suggest that the materials may be taken as an example of a linguistically orientated 'discovery' course, and a statement of a direction in which the language syllabus for native speakers might profitably develop with the help of applied linguistics.

# Appendix

The first page of the test was a pupil's record sheet on which were written the name, class, school, age, place of birth, area of upbringing and details of education.

Text of Test
Overleaf you will find the first page of a short test. Do not begin until your teacher tells you to. Listen carefully to the instructions you are given. Be particularly careful in recording your answers. Write clearly; draw clear lines. If you have to change any answer, make sure your first answer is well crossed out.

**Part A**
Read this passage carefully, at least twice, and try to understand it. Answer the questions below by underlining clearly what you think is the right choice.

> The effect of one language on another, and the effect of dialects on the mother-tongue can account for some changes in pronunciation, but not all. Another cause of pronunciation change that has been suggested is the fact that children grow. The speech organs of children, it is argued, are a different size from adult speech organs; children learn to mimic the noises their parents make, but on their smaller speech organs this really amounts to their using a different instrument. As they grow up, children go on moving their speech organs in the way they learned in their younger days, but the sounds they produce become different as they become adult, because the size of their speech organs is changing. But, if this were true, we should expect all changes of pronunciation to be of the same sort, and this is clearly not the case. This theory also assumes that people stop using their ears to correct their pronunciation after they grow up, which is surely untrue.

1   Which ONE of these statements about the passage is true? Underline it.

a. The passage is mainly concerned with the effects of dialects on the pronunciation of the mother-tongue.
b. The passage is mainly concerned with an argument that children grow up.
c. The passage is mainly concerned with an argument that changes in pronunciation are linked with the adults who make the same speech movements as children, but with different voices.
d. The passage is mainly concerned with the fact that one language does not affect another, and dialects do not affect the pronunciation of the mother-tongue.

2 The author rejects the 'growing child' argument because:
a. Pronunciation changes are not all of the same sort, and adults do not stop using their ears to correct their pronunciation.
b. Speech organs do not grow in the way described.
c. Adult speech organs are the same size as children's, but different in the way they move.
d. Adult size of speech organs and adult movement of speech organs are different from those of a child.

3 When he wrote this passage, the author probably wanted . . .
a. To show that the effect of one language on another and of dialects on the mother-tongue accounted for all changes.
b. To suggest that the growth of children in speaking was out of the question.
c. To discuss briefly and reject one of the arguments people put forward to account for pronunciation changes.
d. To discuss briefly and accept the 'growing child' argument as a valid reason for pronunciation changes.
(Max. time 15 mins.)

End of Part A of test.
*Do not turn over to Part B. Wait until your teacher instructs you.*

## Part B

In this part of the test many of the questions ask you to make a choice of answer from a short list of alternatives. Choose the answer that seems to you to be the most correct one, and *underline it clearly*. If you cannot be absolutely sure of the right answer, choose the one that seems more right than the others. If necessary, guess which answer to choose. You must answer each question. *Example*: Which of the following language patterns is the 'odd man out' (i.e. does not seem similar to the other three).

a. Seven men from Skye
b. All the women from Cyprus
c. <u>Eight soldiers were from Aden</u>
d. Nine boys from Madagascar

Start
The first four questions make use of a tape recorder.

1 Listen carefully to the words that follow, and underline one of the answers listed. We want you to be able to say whether the words you will hear are meant as a question or as a statement. You will hear the words twice. Underline the answer.
*'I was the cause of it.'* (Rising intonation)
a. The words ask a question
b. The words make a statement
c. I cannot tell what the words do

2 Listen carefully to the words on the tape and underline what you think you heard. You will hear the words twice.
a. A man-eating fish
b. A man, eating fish
c. I cannot tell what was said

3 Listen carefully to the words on the tape and underline what you think they meant. 'I didn't do it, because it was difficult.'
a. He finished what he was doing although it was difficult
b. He did not do it because of the difficulty
c. We cannot tell whether he did it or not

4 Listen to the words on the tape and underline clearly what you think you heard.
a. Boys, keep quiet
b. Boys keep quiet
c. We cannot tell which one was said
End of questions on tape.

5 Look at this name: Mr. John Jones
a. Mr. should obviously be spelled 'Mister'.
b. Mr. is the usual way of spelling 'mister' when you write an address on an envelope.

145

c.  Mr. is an abbreviation and good English never uses abbreviations.
d.  Mr. is just a short form of 'Esquire'.

**6**  What makes this a joke?
'An estate agent's assistant, whose job was to write the advertisements for houses for sale, wrote a proposal of marriage to the girl in the office upstairs, — O Eth.wl.y.mry.me? Lf.wd.be.wrthls. wtht.y . . .
a.  He has mis-spelled it all.
b.  He could easily have spoken to her.
c.  He has used the spellings for advertisements for an unusual purpose.
d.  He must be illiterate.

**7**  When we look up the meaning of a word in a good dictionary we find:
a.  The true and only meaning of the word.
b.  The meaning of the word as it would be used by a few highly educated people.
c.  A list of the most common meanings of the word as it is used by speakers of English.
d.  The correct spelling of the word and nothing else.

**8**  How many of the meanings listed below can the phrase 'the bench' take? Underline all possibilities.
a.  The sudden whitening of the skin.
b.  A name for the judge or judges in a court of law.
c.  The padded dual seat of a motor cycle.
d.  A digestive noise.
e.  The work table used by a carpenter.

**9**  How many of the meanings listed below can the phrase 'a hand' take? Underline all possibilities.
a.  A unit of measurement for describing the height of horses.
b.  A hired worker.
c.  A peninsula with sandy shores.
d.  A selection of cards in a card game.
e.  A country word for 'calf'.

**10**  How many of the meanings listed below can the phrase 'a diversion' take? Underline all possibilities.
a.  Part of a coat of arms.

146

b. Two forms of the same story.
c. A road round an obstruction.
d. An amusement, taking your mind off more serious things.
e. A 'road up'.

## Instruction
Different pieces of English can sometimes be shown to be constructed in quite different ways, rather than merely to have different words. In the next group of questions (11–15 inclusive) you will be given a 'family' of four constructions of English, ONE of which is different from the others. This is the 'odd man out'. Underline it.

*Example:*
a. I have flown over the Arctic.
b. You have sailed the seven seas.
c. Don't ever forget this.
d. We have had unforgettable adventures together.
Note : you need not say *why* you choose the answer. Just choose the one you think is the odd man out in the four structures.

**11** Underline the odd man out in these patterns:
a. John will go north.
b. Jean will mend her dress.
c. Tom will have eaten his supper.
d. Bill will read a book.

**12** Underline the odd man out in these patterns:
a. All the cleverest boys.
b. The eight most successful girls.
c. Most of the lazy ones.
d. All my classes are gifted in some way.

**13** Underline the odd man out in these patterns:
a. My old country home in Ireland.
b. Land in the Irish Free State.
c. Our ancient family castle in Kerry.
d. My traditional homeland in the Emerald Isle.

**14** Underline the odd man out in these patterns:
a. I have had a shock.
b. I have been given two tonics.

147

c. One has had no effect.
d. The other has had a little effect.

**15** Underline the odd man out in these patterns:
a. Marvellous fresh country food.
b. I enjoy fresh fruit.
c. Jane loves freshwater fish.
d. We both buy berries.

**16** Choose any ONE of the above 'odd man out' questions (11–15 inclusive) and say in not more than twenty words why you chose your answer.

**17** Here is a language pattern. Look at it carefully and underline in the list given below the piece of language most like it in construction.
Pattern: The tailor made her a good husband.
a. Her husband made her a hamburger.
b. The tailor made him a good suit.
c. The soldier made him a good offer.
d. She made him a splendid servant.

**18** Underline the piece of language in the list most like the pattern given.
Pattern: When I come home, I'll tell you.
a. He came home when he could.
b. When I meet you and talk to you, I'll explain it all.
c. When he reaches London, he'll ring you.
d. I'll tell you when I can find time.

**19** Underline the piece of language in the list most like the pattern given.
Pattern: My old aunt is fit.
a. Her young son is sick.
b. My old aunt has good health.
c. My old school sent me a magazine.
d. The fresh air gave me strength.

**20** An African boy who was learning English wrote this sentence: *An elefant have a long nose.*
Look carefully at his sentence and underline the statement which you think most true of it.
a. The boy has used the right order of words in the sentence.

148

b. The boy has made a mistake in grammar, so his sentence is impossible to understand.
c. The boy has made mistakes in spelling and grammar, so his sentence is impossible to understand.
d. The spelling, the grammar and the order are all wrong in this sentence.

21 Look again at the sentence the African boy wrote, *An elefant have a long nose*. Which of the statements below seems to you to be the most true.
a. You would not expect the word 'nose' to be used in describing an elephant. It should be 'trunk'.
b. 'Long' does not go well with 'nose' when you are describing an elephant.
c. 'Long' comes as a surprise in a description of an elephant's trunk.
d. You cannot make any attempt at all to say what words would be likely to fall with 'elephant' in a description.

22 Here is a quotation. Choose a likely source for it from the list below.
*Quotation:*
'That on copies given away to the author or for the purpose of aiding sale or for review or on copies accidentally destroyed the Publishers shall be free of any liability to pay royalty.'
a. From a friendly letter written by the author to his mother.
b. From a publisher's contract with an author.
c. From a story about the romance of writing.
d. From an author's writing diary.

23 Here is a quotation. Choose a likely source for it from the list below.
*Quotation:*
'Where shall we go?
What is the way to . . . ?
Where does this road lead?
Where can I get a bus to . . . ?'
a. From the words of a traditional song.
b. From a foreign phrase book for travellers.
c. From a travel article describing cheap holidays.
d. From a textbook on polite English tea-table conversation.

**24** Here is a short passage. Read it carefully and note how it is printed. Then choose from the list given below ONE correct statement about it.

*Passage:*

tell you what happened . . . em . . . last summer which . . . eh . . . eh . . . startled me a bit . . . m.eh.n.not . . . em . . . not being . . . em a native of this part . . . em I've not seen many deer . . . and . . . eh . . . when we were walking up this . . . eh . . . eh . . . the Rinns of Kells . . . em . . . there was a big fence . . . and as I as we crossed it . . . a deer ran . . . bounding away.

a. This is what a halting foreigner actually said over the telephone.
b. This is a true piece of ordinary conversation.
c. This is the conversation of an illiterate speaker.
d. This cannot be conversation because you cannot understand it.

End of Part B of the Test.

When you finish, *do not go back over your answers and do not alter anything*. Put your pencil down and wait quietly for the others to finish.

# Bibliography

Abercrombie, D. (1965) *Studies in Phonetics and Linguistics*, London
    (1967) *Elements of General Phonetics*, Edinburgh
Albrow, K. H. (1968) *The Rhythm and Intonation of Spoken English*,
    Paper No. 9, Programme in Linguistics and English Teaching, London
Allen, W. S. (1957) *On the Linguistic Study of Languages*, Cambridge; in
    Strevens (ed.) (1966) 1–26
Allen, J. P. B. and van Buren, P. (1971) *Chomsky: Selected Readings*,
    London
Andrews, S. O. (1923) *The Teaching of Grammar*, English Association
    Pamphlet, No. 56, London, 1923
Austin, C. A. (1927) 'The Laboratory Method in Teaching Geometry',
    *Mathematics Teacher*, 1927, 20, 286–294
Ausubel, D. P. (1961) 'Learning by Discovery: Rationale and Mystique',
    *Bull. Nat. Assoc. Sec. Sch. Princ.*, Vol. 45, 1961, 18–58
    (1963) *The Psychology of Meaningful Verbal Learning*, London
Bain, A. (1869) *English Composition and Rhetoric*, London
    (1887) *On Teaching English*, London
Barber, C. (1964a) *Linguistic Change in Present Day English*, London
    (1964b) *The Story of Language*, London
Barclay, J. and Knox, D. H. (1962) *Approach to Standard English*, Glasgow
Beard, R. M. (1957) *An Investigation of Concept Formation among Infant
    School Children*, Ph.D. Thesis, London University (Unpublished)
Bellugi, U. and Brown, R. (eds.) (1964) *The Acquisition of Language*,
    Monograph of the Society for Research in Child Development, Serial
    No. 92, Vol. 29, No. 1
Bernstein, B. (1965) 'A Socio-linguistic Approach to Social Learning', in
    Penguin *Survey of Social Sciences*, 1965, London
Betts, E. A. (1934) 'An Evaluation of Certain Techniques for the Study of Oral
    Composition', *Res. Stud. Elem. Sch. Lang.*, No. 1. Univ. Iowa. Stud.
    Educ., 9, No. 2, 7–35, in Travis, (1957)
Blair, H. (1783) *Lectures on Rhetoric and Belles Lettres*, Edinburgh
Bloch, B. and Trager, G. L. (1942) *Outline of Linguistic Analysis*, Baltimore
Bloomfield, L. (1925) 'Why a Linguistic Society?', *Lg.* I, 1–5
    (1933) *Language*, New York
Board of Education (1941) *Curriculum and Examinations in Secondary
    Schools*, Report of the Committee of the Secondary School Examinations
    Council Appointed by the President of the Board of Education in 1941,
    (The Norwood Report), H.M.S.O., London
Bolinger, D. (1964) 'Around the Edge of Language: Intonation', *H.E.R.*,
    Vol. 34, No. 2, 1964, 282–296

Boomer, D. S. (1965) 'Hesitation and Grammatical Encoding', *Lang. and Sp.*, Vol. 8, Pt. 3, 1965, 148–158

Boomer, D. S. and Dittman, A. T. (1962) 'Hesitation Pauses and Juncture Pauses in Speech', *Lang. and Sp.*, Vol. 5, Pt. 4, 1962, 215–220

Borgh, E. M. (1963) *Grammatical Patterns and Composition,* Wisconsin

Bowden, T. C. (*et al.*) (1963) *The Macmillan English Series*, New York

Bowen, J. D. (1966) 'A Multiple Register Approach to Teaching English', *Estudios Linguisticos Revista Brasileira de Linguistica Teorica e Applicada*, Vol. 1, No. 2 Dezembro, 1966

Boyd, J. and Thorne, J. P. (1969) 'The Semantics of Modal Verbs', *J.L.*, 5, 57–74

Bright, J. A. (1947) 'Grammar in the English Syllabus', *E.L.T.,* in Lee (ed.) (1967a) 21–25

Brown, E. K. (1968) 'Review of Bailey (1968) "Jamaican Creole Syntax" ', *J.L.*, Vol. 4, No. 2, 296–298

Brown, R. W. (1956) *Language and Categories*, in Bruner, Goodnow and Austin, (1956)

Brown, R. and Fraser, C. (1964) *The Acquisition of Syntax*, in Bellugi and Brown (1964) 43–47

Bruner, J. S. (1957) *Going Beyond the Information Given*, in Colorado Symposium, (1957)

(1960) *The Process of Education*, Harvard

(1961) 'The Act of Discovery', *H.E.R.*, 31, 21–32

(*et al.*) (1965) *Studies in Cognitive Growth*, London

(1966) *On Knowing, Essays for the Left Hand*, Harvard

(1967) *Towards a Theory of Instruction*, Harvard

Bruner, J. S., Goodnow, J. J. and Austin, G. A. (1956) *A Study of Thinking*, New York

van Buren, P. (1966) *An Approach to the Description of Child-Speech*, Mimeo, Department of Child Life and Health, Edinburgh University

(1967) *Ontogenesis of an Approach to the Description of Child-Speech*, Mimeo. Paper read at a Seminar on Child Language, May 1967, Dept. of Child Life and Health, Edinburgh University

Campbell, G. (1776) *The Philosophy of Rhetoric*, London

Cane, B. (ed.) (1967) *Research into Teacher Education*, National Foundation for Educational Research in England and Wales, Slough

Carmichael, L. (1964) *The Early Growth of Language Capacity in the Individual*, in Lenneberg (1964), 1–22

Carroll, J. B. (1953) *The Study of Language*, Harvard

(1960) 'Language Development in Children', in Saporta (ed.) (1961) 331–345

Catford, J. C. (1965) *A Linguistic Theory of Translation*, London

Cattell, N. R. (1966) *The Design of English*, Melbourne

Chao, Y. R. (1968) *Language and Symbolic Systems*, London

Cherry, C. (1963) *On Human Communication*, New York

Chomsky, N. (1957) *Syntactic Structures*, The Hague

(1959) 'Review of Skinner's "Verbal Behavior" ', (1957), *Lg.*, 35, 26–58;

in Fodor and Katz (1964), 547–578

(1961) 'Some Methodological Remarks on Generative Grammar', *Word*, 17, 219–239

(1962) *The Logical Basis of Linguistic Theory*, in Proceedings of the Ninth International Congress of Linguistics, Cambridge, Mass., 1962

(1964) *Current Issues in Linguistic Theory*, The Hague

(1965) *Aspects of the Theory of Syntax*, M.I.T.

(1966a) *Topics in the Theory of Generative Grammar*, The Hague

(1966b) *Cartesian Linguistics*, M.I.T.

(1966c) 'Linguistic Theory', in *Language Teaching: Broader Contexts*, Reports of the Working Committees (R. J. Mead, Jr., ed.) of the Northeast Conference on the Teaching of Foreign Languages, M.L.A., New York

(1968a) 'A Universal Grammar', B.B.C. Third Programme discussion with Stuart Hampshire, reprinted in *The Listener*, Vol. 79, No. 2044, 30th May 1968

(1968b) *Language and Mind*, New York

Christensen, F. (1967) *Notes Towards a New Rhetoric*, London

Clark, R. (1967) *Case Grammar and the Psychologist*, D.A.L. Edinburgh (Work Paper)

Classification of Occupations (1966) H.M.S.O., London

Clegg, A. B. (ed.) (1964) *The Excitement of Writing*, London

Cobbett, W. (1826) *A Grammar of the English Language in a Series of Letters, intended for the Use of Schools and of Young Persons in General; but more especially for use of Soldiers, Sailors, Apprentices and Plough-boys*, London

Conlin, D. A. and Herman, G. R. (1965) *Modern Grammar and Composition, Grade 12*, New York

Colorado Symposium (1957) *Contemporary Approaches to Cognition*, Cambridge, (Mass.)

Corder, S. P. (1960) *English Language Teaching and Television*, London

(1966) *The Visual Element in Language Teaching*, London

Craig, R. C. (1953) *The Transfer Value of Guided Learning*, Columbia University, New York

(1956) 'Directed v. Independent Discovery of Established Relations', *Jour. Educ. Psy.*, Vol. 47, 1956, 223–234

Crystal, D. and Quirk, R. (1965) *Prosodic and Paralinguistic Systems in English*, The Hague

Currie, W. B. (1965a) *Some Applications of Linguistics in the Training of Specialist Teachers of English*, Dissertation in Department of Applied Linguistics, Edinburgh University (Unpublished)

(1965b) 'Linguistics, The Teacher and the Syllabus', *Dominie*, December 1965

(1966) 'The Language Performance of Certificate Candidates', *Bulletin of Glasgow Corporation Education Department*, May 1966, 3–6

(1967a) 'Applying Linguistics', *S.S.T.A. Mag.*, June 1967

(1967b) *Discovering Language V*, London

(1969) Discovering Language II, London

(1968) 'Richness of English: Rhetoric in a New Key', *T.E.S.* (Scot.), 3rd May 1968, 1461

Davie, G. E. (1961) *The Democratic Intellect*, Edinburgh

Davies, A. (1965) *Linguistics and Teaching Spoken English*, in Wilkinson (ed.) (1965), 17–39

(1968) 'Language Varieties in Teaching', in *The Place of Language*, *Educ. Rev.*, Vol. 20, No. 2, Feb. 1968, 107–122

Davies, E. (1968a) *Aspects of General Linguistics*, Paper No. 8, Programme in Linguistics and English Teaching, London

(1968b) *Elements of English Clause Structure*, Paper No. 10, Programme in Linguistics and English Teaching, London

Della-Piana, G. (1957) 'Searching Orientation and Concept Learning', *Jour. Educ. Psy.*, Vol. 48, 1957, 244 ff.

Diack, H. (1956) 'A Re-examination of Grammar', *The Use of English*, Vol. 7. No. 4, 1956, in Wilson (ed.) (1967) 152–157

Dineen, F. P. (1967) *An Introduction to General Linguistics*, New York

Dixon, J. (1967) *Growth Through English*, N.A.T.E., Reading

Dixon, R. (1964) *Linguistic Science and Logic*, The Hague

(1965) *What is Language?*, London

Doughty, P. (1968a) *The Relevance of Linguistics for the Teacher of English*, Paper No. 1, Programme in Linguistics and English Teaching, London

(1968b) *Current Attitudes to Written English, and their Implications for the Teacher of English*, Paper No. 4, Programme (as above)

(1968c) *Linguistics and the Teaching of Literature*, Paper No. 5, Programme (as above)

(1971) *Language in Use*, Arnold, 1971

Dubber, A. W. S. (no date) *Interpretation and Language Exercises*, Glasgow

Dykema, K. (1962) 'Progress in Grammar', *Coll. Eng.*, Vol. 14, No. 2, 1952, 93–100

Ebel, R. L. (1965) *Measuring Educational Achievement*, Engelwood Cliffs

Edinburgh Corporation Education Committee (1947) *Schemes of Work for Primary Schools*, Edinburgh

English Association Pamphlet No. 56 (1923)

English Association Pamphlet No. 75 (1930)

Enkvist, N. E., Spencer, J. and Gregory, M. J. (1964) *Linguistics and Style*, London

Ervin, S. M. (1964) *Imitation and Structural Change in Children's Language*, in Lenneberg (1964) 163–192

Esper, E. A. (1968) *Mentalism and Objectivism in Linguistics*, New York

Fillmore, C. J. (1967) *The Case for Case*, Proceedings of the 1967 Texas Conference on Language Universals, Bach and Harms (eds.) (1968)

Firth, J. R. (1935) 'The Techniques of Semantics', *T.P.S.*, 1935, 36–72 in Firth (1964) 7–34

(1937) *The Tongues of Men and Speech*, reprinted 1964, London

(1957) *Synopsis of Linguistic Theory*, Oxford

(1964) *Papers in Linguistics*, 1934–1951, Oxford (First published 1959)

Fisher, R. A. (1935) *Design of Experiments*, Edinburgh

154

Flower, F. D. (1966) *Language and Education*, London

Fodor, J. and Garrett, M. (1966) *Some Reflections on Competence and Performance*, in Lyons and Wales (eds.) (1966) 135–154

Fowler, H. W. (1926) *Modern English Usage*, London

Francis, W. N. (1954) 'Revolution in Grammar', *Quar. Jour. Speech*, Vol. 40, Oct. 1954, 299–312

Fraser, H. (1965) *A Basis for Composition*, Dissertation in Dept. of Applied Linguistics, Edinburgh University (Unpublished)

(1967) *Control and Create*, London

Fraser, H. and O'Donnell, W. R. (eds.) (1969) *Applied Linguistics and the Teaching of English*, London

Fries, C. C. (1927) *The Teaching of the English Language*, New York

(1940) *American English Grammar*, New York

(1952) *The Structure of English*, New York

(1954) 'Meaning and Linguistic Analysis', *Lang.*, Vol. 30, 1, 1954, 57–6

(1962) *Linguistics and Reading*, New York

Froome, S. (1970) *Why Tommy isn't Learning*, Tom Stacey, London

Frye, N. (1963) *The Well-tempered Critic*, Bloomington

(1964) 'Criticism, Visible and Invisible', *Coll. Eng.*, Vol. 26, No. 1, Oct 1964, 3–12

Gage, N. L. (ed.) (1964) *Handbook of Research on Teaching*, Chicago

Glasgow Corporation Education Committee (1966) *Syllabus for Spoken English*, Glasgow

Gleason, H. A., Jr. (1955) *An Introduction to Descriptive Linguistics*, New York

(1964) 'What Grammar?', *H.E.R.*, Vol. 34, No. 2, 1964

(1965) *Linguistics and English Grammar*, New York

Goldman-Eisler, F. (1961) *Hesitation and Information in Speech*, Paper for 4th London Conference on Information Theory, 1961

(1968) *Experiments in Spontaneous Speech*, New York

Grattan, J. H. G. and Gurrey, P. (1930) *Our Language*, London

Gregory, M. (1967) 'Aspects of Varieties Differentiation', *J.L.*, Vol. 3, No. 2, 1967, 177–198

Grierson, H. J. C. (1944) *Rhetoric and English Composition*, Edinburgh

Hall, R. A., Jr. (1950) *Leave Your Language Alone!*, New York

(1960) *Linguistics and Your Language*, New York. Revision of Hall (1950)

Halliday, M. A. K. (1961) 'Categories of the Theory of Grammar', *Word*, Vol. 17, No. 3, Dec. 1961

(1963a) 'The Tones of English', *Arch. L.*, 15, 1–28

(1963b) 'Intonation and English Grammar', *T.P.S.*, 1963, 143–169

(1963c) 'Class in Relation to Chain and Choice', *Ling.*, 2, 5–15

(1964a) *Syntax and the Consumer*, in C. I. J. M. Stuart (ed.) Report of the Fifteenth Annual (First International) Round Table Meeting on Linguistics and Language Studies, Monograph Series on Languages and Linguistics, 17, Washington, D.C., Georgetown University Press, 11–14

(1964b) (With A. McIntosh and P. D. Strevens) *The Linguistic Sciences and Language Teaching*, London

(1965) *Linguistics and the Teaching of English*, Work Paper, Mimeo

(1966a) 'Patterns in Words', Reprint of B.B.C. Third Programme broadcast, *The Listener*, 13th Jan. 1966

(1966b) 'Some Notes on "Deep" Grammar', *J.L.*, Vol. 2, No. 1, 1966 57–67

(1966c) 'The Concept of Rank: A Reply', *J.L.*, Vol. 2, No. 1, 1966, 110–118

(1966d) *The English Verbal Group: A Specimen of a Manual of Analysis*, Nuffield Project in Linguistics, and English Teaching, Work Paper VI, 1966

(1966e) (With A. McIntosh) *Patterns of Language*, London

(1966f) *Lexis as a Linguistic Level*, in Bazell (*et al.*) (eds.) (1966), 148–162

(1967a) *Some Aspects of the Thematic Organisation of the English Clause*, RAND Corporation. (Memorandum RM – 5224 – PR)

(1967b) *Intonation and Grammar in British English*, The Hague

(1967c) *Grammar, Society and the Noun*, (Inaugural Lecture, University College, London, 24th Nov. 1966), London

(1967d) *Language and Experience*. A Paper read to the Nursery School Association Conference on Children's Problems in Language, Harrogate, 1967, Mimeo.

(1967e) 'Notes on Transitivity and Theme in English', Part 1, *J.L.*, Vol. 3, No. 1, 37–81

(1967f) 'Notes on Transitivity and Theme', Part 2, *J.L.*, Vol. 3, No. 2, 199–244

(1968a) 'Notes on Transitivity and Theme in English', Part 3, *J.L.*, Vol. 4, No. 2, 179–215

(1968b) *Introduction to Intonation* (Part of a Course in Spoken English, with R. Mackin, K. H. Albrow and J. McH. Sinclair) Oxford

(1968c) *Introduction* to Papers of the Programme in Linguistics and English Teaching, London; in Paper No. 1. (See Doughty, 1968a)

(1969) *Options and Functions in the English Clause*, BRNO Studies, etc.

(1971) *Language in a Social Perspective* Educ. Rev. 23, No. 3.

Hamp, E. P. (1960) 'General Linguistics – The United States in the Fifties', in *Trends in European Linguistics, 1930–1960*, Ninth International Congress of Linguists, Utrecht

Harris, C. W. (ed.) (1960) *Encyclopedia of Educational Research*, New York

Harris, R. J. (1965) 'The Only Disturbing Feature', *The Use of English*, XVI, 197–202

Harris, Z. S. (1951) *Methods in Structural Linguistics*, Chicago

(1961) *Structural Linguistics*, Chicago. (Reprint of Harris, 1951)

Hasan, R. (1968) *Grammatical Cohesion in Spoken and Written English, Part 1*, Paper 7 in Programme in Linguistics and English Teaching, London

Hasan, R. and Lushington, S. (1968) *The Subject Matter of English*, Paper

No. 2 in Programme (as above)

Haselrud, G. M. and Meyers, S. (1958) 'The Transfer Value of Given and Individually Derived Principles', *Jour. Ed. Psy.*, Vol. 49, 1958, 293–298

Haugen, E. (1951) 'Directions in Modern Linguistics', *Lg.*, Vol. 27, No. 3, 1951

Hendrix, G. (1947) 'A New Clue to Transfer of Training', *Elem. Sch. Jour.*, XLVIII, 4; Dec. 1947, 197–208

Hill, A. A. (1958) *Introduction to Linguistic Structures*, New York

Hockett, C. (1954) 'Two Models of Grammatical Description', *Word*, Vol. 10, No. 2, 1954, 210–234

Hodgson, W. B. (1882) *Errors in the Use of English*, Edinburgh

Holbrook, D. (1964) *English for Maturity*, London

Hoyt, F. S. (1906) 'The Place of Grammar in the Elementary Curriculum', *Teachers' College Record*, Vol. 8, Nov. 1906

Huddleston, R. D. (1965) 'Rank and Depth', *Lg.*, 41, 574–586

Hudson, R. A. (1967) 'Constituency in a Systemic Description of the English Clause', *Lingua*, 17

Hunter, S. L. (1968) *The Scottish Educational System*, London

Hutton, P. E. M., Rintoul, D. and McKinnon, W. T. (1962) *Ordinary English*, London

Huxley, R. (1966) *Suggestions for the Description of Child Language, Part 1*, Mimeo. Department of Child Life and Health, University of Edinburgh

Ingram, E. (1968) *Review* of Smith and Miller (1966) and Lyons and Wales (1966), 'Recent Trends in Psycholinguistics: A Critical Notice', (1969) *Brit. Jour. Psychol.*, Vol. 53, No. 3, 1969, 315–325

Ingram, T. (1966) *Annual Report* of the Nuffield Foundation Language Development Research Project in the Department of Child Life and Health, University of Edinburgh. (Mimeo)

Irving, D. (1809) *The Elements of English Composition*, London

Ivic, M. (1965) *Trends in Linguistics*, The Hague

Jacobs, R. A. and Rosenbaum, P. S. (1967a) *Grammar 1*, Boston
(1967b) *Grammar 2*, Boston

Jagger, H. J. (1960) *A Handbook of English Grammar*, London

Jakobson, R. (1941) *Kindersprache, Aphasie, und allgemeine Lautgesetze*, Uppsala
(1960) *Linguistics and Poetics*, in Sebeok (ed.) (1960)
(1968) *Child Language, Aphasia and Phonological Universals*, The Hague, Translation of (1941)

Jespersen, O. (1922) *Language: Its Nature, Development and Origin*, New York
(1924) *The Philosophy of Grammar*, London
(1928) *Modern English Grammar*, Heidelberg
(1933) *Essentials of English Grammar*, London
(1964) *Mankind, Nation and Individual from a Linguistic Point of View*, Bloomington

Joos, M. (1962) *The Five Clocks*, The Hague

Kames, Lord (1762) *The Elements of Criticism*, London

157

Katona, G. (1940) *Organising and Memorizing*, Columbus University, New York

Katz, J. J. and Fodor, J. A. (1963) 'The Structure of a Semantic Theory', *Lg.*, 39, 170–210 in Fodor and Katz (eds.) (1964) 479–518

Katz, J. J. and Postal, P. (1964) *An Integrated Theory of Linguistic Description*, M.I.T.

Kerr, W. (1932) *The English Apprentice*, London

Kersh, B. Y. (1958) 'The Adequacy of "Meaning" as an Explanation for the Superiority of Learning by Independent Discovery', *Jour. Educ. Psy.*, Vol. 44, 1958, 282–292

    (1962) 'The Motivating Effect of Learning by Directed Discovery', *Jour. Educ. Psy.*, Vol. 53, No. 2, 1962, 65–71

Kittell, J. E. (1957) 'An Experimental Study of the Effect of External Guidance on Transfer and Retention of Principles', *Jour. Educ. Psy.*, Vol. 48, 1957, 391–405

Klima, E. S. and Bellugi, U. (1966) *Syntactic Regularities in the Speech of Children*, in Lyons and Wales, (1966) 183–208

Kreidler, C. W. (1966) 'The Influence of Linguistics in School Grammar', *Ling. Rep.*, Vol. 8, No. 6, 1966, 1–4

Kruisinga, E. (1917) *A Handbook of Present Day English*, Utrecht

Labov, W. (1966) *The Social Stratification of English in New York City*, Center of Applied Linguistics, Washington

Lamb, P. (1967) *Linguistics in Proper Perspective*, Columbus

Lamb, S. (1964) *On Alternation, Transformation, Realisation and Stratification*. In C. I. J. M. Stuart (ed.) Report of the Fifteenth Annual, (First International) Round Table Meeting on Linguistics and Language Studies, Monograph Series on Language and Linguistics, 17, Georgetown, 105–122

    (1966) *Outline of Stratificational Grammar*, Georgetown

Lambert, W. E. (1967) *A Social Psychology of Bilingualism*, (Mimeo.) Jour. Soc. Issues, (Forthcoming)

Langendoen, D. T. (1968) *The London School of Linguistics: A Study of the Linguistic Theories of B. Malinowski and J. R. Firth*, M.I.T.

Langer, S. (1949) Philosophy in a New Key, London

Lashley, K. S. (1951) *The Problem of Serial Order in Behavior*, in Cerebral Mechanisms in Behavior, L. A. Jeffress (ed.) New York, and in Saporta (ed.) (1961) 180–198

Laver, J. (1970) The Production of Speed, in Lyons (ed.) New Horizons in Linguistics, London

Lee, W. R. (ed.) (1967a) *E.L.T. Selections 1*, London

    (1967b) *E.L.T. Selections 2*, London

Leech, G. (1964) 'Advertising's Grammar', *New Society*, 8th Oct. 1964

Lees, R. B. (1957) 'Review of Chomsky's "Syntactic Structures" (1957)', *Lg.*, Vol. 33, July–Sept. 1957, 275–408

    (1964) 'Formal Discussion' of Brown and Fraser (1964) and Brown, Fraser and Bellugi (1964) in *The Acquisition of Language*, Monograph of the Society for Research in Child Development, Vol. 29, No. 1, 1964, 92–98

(1965) 'Two Views of Linguistic Research', *Ling.,* Vol. 11, Jan., 1965, 21–29

Lenneberg, E. J. (ed.) (1964) *New Directions in the Study of Language,* M.I.T.

Leroy, M. (1967) *The Main Trends in Modern Linguistics,* Oxford

Levin, S. R. (1960) 'Comparing Traditional and Structural Grammar', *Coll. Eng.,* Vol. 21, Feb. 1960, 260–275

Lewis, M. M. (1936) *Infant Speech,* London

Longacre, R. E. (1960) 'String Constituent Analysis', *Lg.,* Vol. 36, No. 1, 1960, 63–88

Lunzer, E. A. (1960) 'Some Points of Piagetian Theory in the Light of Experimental Criticism', *Jour. Ch. Psychol. and Psychiatry,* Vol. 1, No. 3, 1960

Luria and Yudovich (1959) Speech and the Development of Mental Processes in the Child, London

Lyons, J. (1963) *Structural Semantics,* London

  (1966a) *Firth's Theory of Meaning,* in Bazell (*et al.*) (eds.) (1966) 288–302

  (1966b) 'Towards a "Notional" Theory of the "Parts of Speech" ', *J.L.,* Vol. 2, No. 2, (1966), 209–236

  (1968) *Introduction to Theoretical Linguistics,* London

  (1970) *Chomsky,* London

Lyons, J. and Wales (eds.) (1966) *Psycholinguistic Papers,* Edinburgh

Macauley, D. (1969) *Some Approaches to the Study of Language,* in Fraser and O'Donnell (eds.) (1969) (Forthcoming)

Macauley, W. J. (1947) 'The Difficulty of Grammar', *Brit. Jour. Educ. Psy.,* Vol. XVIII, 1947

McCarthy, D. (1930) *The Language Development of the Preschool Child,* Inst. of Child Welfare Monograph Series No. 4, Minnesota

McIntosh, A. (1961a) 'Patterns and Ranges', *Lg.,* Vol. 37, No. iii, 1961, 325–337, also in McIntosh and Halliday (1966) 183–199

  (1961b) ' "Graphology" and Meaning', *Arch. L.,* Vol. XIII, Fasc. 2, 107–120

  (1965) 'Saying', *Rev. Eng. Lit.,* Vol. VI, No. 2, 1965, 9–20

McIntosh, A. and Halliday, M. A. K. (1966) *Patterns of Language: Papers in General, Descriptive and Applied Linguistics,* London

Mackay, D. and Thompson, B. (1968) *The Initial Teaching of Reading and Writing,* Paper No. 3, in Programme in Linguistics, and English Teaching, London

Mackey, W. F. (1965) *Language Teaching Analysis,* London

McNeill, D. (1966a) *Developmental Psycholinguistics,* in Smith and Miller (eds.) (1966), 15–83

  (1966b) *The Creation of Language by Children,* in Lyons and Wales (eds.) (1966), 99–120

  (1966c) 'The Creation of Language', *Discovery,* Vol. 27, No. 7 (1966), 34–38; also in Oldfield and Marshall (eds.) (1968) 21–31

Marckwardt, A. H. (1965) 'Linguistics Issue: An Introduction', *Coll. Eng.,* Vol. 26, No. 4, Jan. 1965, 249–254

(1966) *Linguistics and the Teaching of English*, London

Marshall, J. C. and Wales, R. J. (1966) 'Which Syntax : A Consumer's Guide', *J.L.*, Vol. 2, No. 2, (1966), 181–188

Martin, T. (1961) *The Instructed Vision*, Bloomington

Matthews, P. (1966) 'The Concept of Rank in "Neo-Firthian" Grammar' *J.L.*, Vol. 2, No. 1, (1966), 101–110

(1967) 'Review of Chomsky's "Aspects" (1965)', *J.L.*, Vol. 3, No. 1, (1967), 119–152

Mawer, A. (1923) *The Problem of Grammar in the Light of Modern Linguistic Thought*, in English Association Pamphlet No. 56, London, 1923

May, L. W. M. (1967) *Outline of a Modern Grammar of English*, Glasgow

Mead, R. J. (ed.) (1966) *Language Teaching: Broader Contexts*. (See Chomsky, 1966) Reports of the Working Committees of the Northeast Conference on the Teaching of Foreign Languages, 1966, M.L.A., New York

Mende, R. A. (*et al.*) (1961) *Effective English*, New York

Miller, G. A. (1951) *Language and Communication*, New York

(1964) *Language and Psychology*, in Lenneberg (1964), 89–108

Miller, G. A., Galanter, E. and Pribram, K. H. (1960) *Plans and the Structure of Behavior*, New York

Miller, K. M. (1957) 'Einstellung Rigidity, Intelligence and Teaching Methods', *Brit. Jour. Educ. Psy.*, Vol. 27 (1957), 127–134

Ministry of Education (1954) *Language: Some Suggestions for Teachers of English and Others in Primary and Secondary Schools and in Further Education*, Pamphlet No. 26, H.M.S.O., London

Mittins, W. H. (1959) *The Teaching of English in Schools*, in Quirk and Smith (eds.) (1959) 106–132

(1962) *A Grammar of Modern English*, London

Moulton, W. G. (1966) *A Linguistic Guide to Language Learning*, M.L.A., New York

Mussen, R. H. (1963) *The Psychological Development of the Child*, Englewood Cliffs

National Foundation for Educational Research in England and Wales (1968) *Research into Teacher Education*. Report of a Conference held 4th July 1967. B. Cane (ed.) *q.v.* Slough

National Froebel Foundation (1960–61) *Piaget's Findings and the Teacher*, London

National Union of Teachers (1952) *The Curriculum of the Secondary School*, London

Nesfield, J. C. (1912) *Modern English Grammar*, London

(1898) *Manual of English Grammar and Composition*, London

Nesfield, J. C. and Wood, F. T. (1964) *Manual of English Grammar and Composition*, London

Newsome, V. L. (1961) *Structural Grammar in the Classroom*, Milwaukee

Nichols, M. H. (1963) *Rhetoric and Criticism*, New York

Nida, E. A. (1960) *A Synopsis of English Syntax*, Oklahoma

(1966) *A Synopsis of English Syntax*, The Hague

160

Norwood (See Board of Education)

Nuffield Foundation Foreign Languages Teaching Materials Project (1964) *The Language of Eight-year-old Children* (Recorded by R. Hasen) Reports and Occasional Papers No. 5, Leeds

Ohmann, R. (1964) 'In Lieu of a New Rhetoric', *Coll. Eng.,* Vol. 26, No. 1, Oct., 1964, 17–22

Oldfield, R. C. and Marshall, J. C. (eds.) (1968) *Language: Selected Readings,* London

O'Neil, W. A. (1968) *Paul Roberts' Rules of Order: The Misuses of Linguistics in the Classroom,* The Urban Review, June 1968, 12–16

Osborne, G. S. (1966) *Scottish and English Schools,* London

Palmer, F. R. (1965) *A Linguistic Study of the English Verb,* London

Palmer, H. E. (1933) *A New Classification of English Tones,* Tokyo

(1964) *The Principles of Language Study,* London. (First published 1921)

Patrick, M. (1949) *Four Centuries of Scottish Psalmody,* London

Pei, M. A. and Gaynor, F. (1954) *Dictionary of Linguistics,* London

Philip, A. (1968) *Attitudes to Correctness in English: A Linguistic View of Language in Use.* Paper No. 6, Programme in Linguistics and English Teaching, London

Pilliner, A. E. G. (1968) *Examinations,* Bulletin of the University of Edinburgh, June 1968

Pink, M. A. (1954) *An Outline of English Grammar,* London

Pooley, R. C. (1957) *Teaching of English Grammar,* New York

Postal, P. (1964a) 'Underlying and Superficial Linguistic Structure', *H.E.R.,* Vol. 34, No. 2, (1964), 246–266

(1964b) *Constituent Structure,* The Hague

Postman, N. (1963–66) *The New English,* New York

Postman, N., Morine, H. and Morine, G. (1963) *Discovering Your Language,* New York

Poutsma, H. (1914) *A Grammar of Late Modern English,* Gröningen

Pride, J. B. (1971) *The Social Meaning of Language,* London

Proceedings of the Classical Association (1908)

de Quincey, T. (1860) 'Critical Suggestions on Style and Rhetoric', in *Selections Brave and Gay,* 1853–60

Quirk, R. (1959) *English Language and the Structural Approach,* in Quirk and Smith (eds.) (1959) 13–46

(1962) *The Use of English,* London

Quirk, R. and Smith, A. H. (eds.) (1959) *The Teaching of English, Studies in Communication,* London

Rapeer, L. W. (1913) 'The Problem of Formal Grammar in Elementary Education', *Jour. Educ. Psy.,* Vol. 4, March 1913

Richards, I. A. (1936) *The Philosophy of Rhetoric,* New York

Rivers, W. (1968) 'Grammar in Foreign Language Teaching', *M.L.J.,* April 1968, 205–211

Robbie, H. J. L. and Hutton, P. E. M. (1955) *English Principles and Practice,* London

161

Roberts, P. (1956) *Patterns of English*, New York
    (1960) 'The Relation of Linguistics to the Teaching of English', *Coll. Eng.*, Vol. 22, Oct. 1960, 1–9 ; in Wilson (ed.) (1967) 27–36
    (1962) *English Sentences*, New York
    (1964) *English Syntax*, New York (Alternate Version)
    (1966) *The Roberts English Series: A Linguistic Programme, Grades 3–6*, New York
    (1967a) *The Roberts English Series: A Linguistic Programme, Grade 7*, New York
    (1967b) *Modern Grammar*, New York
Roberts, A. E. and Barter, A. (1908) *The Teaching of English*, London
Robins, R. H. (1951) *Ancient and Mediaeval Grammatical Theory in Europe*, London
    (1964) *General Linguistics, An Introductory Survey*, London
    (1967) *A Short History of Linguistics*, London
Robinson, N. (1960) 'The Relation between Knowledge of English Grammar and Ability in Composition', *Brit. Jour. Educ. Psy.*, Vol. XXX, 1960
Rogovin, S. (1964) *Modern English Sentence Structure*, New York
Rosenberg, S. (ed.) (1965) *Directions in Psycholinguistics*, New York
Saporta, S. (ed.) (1961) *Psycholinguistics*, New York
    (1966) 'Applied Linguistics and Generative Grammar', in Valdman (ed.) (1966) *Trends in Language Teaching*, New York
Saporta, S., Blumenthal, A. L., Lockowski, P. and Reiff, D. G. (1965) *Grammatical Models and Language Learning*, in Rosenberg (ed.) (1965) 15–28
de Saussure, F. (1916) *Cours de Linguistique Générale*, Paris
    (1959) *Course in General Linguistics*, New York
Scaiola, M. G. (1965) *An Introductory Programme to the Nominal Group*, Dissertation, Department of Applied Linguistics, Edinburgh University. (Unpublished)
Schools Council, (1965) *Mathematics in Primary Schools*, H.M.S.O., London
Schools Council (1965) *English: A Programme for Research and Development in English Teaching*, Working Paper No. 3, H.M.S.O., London
    (1967) *The New Curriculum*, H.M.S.O., London
    (1971) *Language in Use*, H.M.S.O., London
Scotch Education Department (1895) *Annual Reports*, H.M.S.O., Edinburgh
    (1900) *Annual Reports*, H.M.S.O., Edinburgh
Scott, F. S. (*et al.*) (1968) *English Grammar – A Linguistic Study of its Classes and Structures*
Scottish Education Department
    (1907) Annual Reports, H.M.S.O., Edinburgh
    (1908) Annual Reports, H.M.S.O., Edinburgh
    (1913) Annual Reports, H.M.S.O., Edinburgh
    (1924) Annual Reports, H.M.S.O., Edinburgh
    (1927) Annual Reports, H.M.S.O., Edinburgh
    (1946) *Primary Education*, A Report of the Advisory Council on Education

in Scotland, H.M.S.O., Edinburgh, Cmd. 6973

(1947) *Secondary Education*, A Report of the Advisory Council on Education in Scotland, H.M.S.O., Edinburgh, Cmd. 7005

(1952) *English in Secondary Schools*, H.M.S.O., Edinburgh

(1954) *Reading in the Primary School*, H.M.S.O., Edinburgh

(1955) *Junior Secondary Education*, H.M.S.O., Edinburgh

(1956a) *Composition in the Primary School*, H.M.S.O., Edinburgh

(1956b) *Report on the Teaching of English in Secondary Schools*, H.M.S.O., Edinburgh

(1962) *New Ways in Junior Secondary Education*, H.M.S.O., Edinburgh

(1965) *Primary Education in Scotland*, H.M.S.O., Edinburgh

(1967) *English in the Secondary School: Early Stages*, Bulletin No. 1 of the Central Committee on English, H.M.S.O., Edinburgh

(1968) *The Teaching of Literature*, Bulletin No. 2 of the Central Committee on English, H.M.S.O., Edinburgh

Sebeok, T. A. (ed.) (1960) *Style in Language*, M.I.T.

Segel, J. and Barr, J. (1926) 'Relation of Achievement in Formal Grammar to Achievement in Applied Grammar', *Jour. Educ. Res.*, Vol. XIV, Dec. 1926

Simpson, I. J. (1947) *Education in Aberdeenshire before 1872*, London

Sinclair, J. M. (1965) *The Edinburgh Course of Spoken English Grammar*, London

(1966a) *Beginning the Study of Lexis*, in Bazell (*et al.*) (eds.) (1966) 410–430

(1966b) *What does the Teacher need to know about the Structure of the English Language?* Working Paper No. 11, Dartmouth Seminar, 1966 (Unpublished)

(1968) 'English Language in English Studies', *Educ. Rev.*, Vol. 20, No. 2, Feb. 1968

(1972) *A Course in Spoken English: Grammar*, London

Skeat, W. W. (1891) *Principles of English Etymology*, London

Skinner, B. F. (1957) *Verbal Behavior*, New York

Sledd, J. (1955) 'Review of "The Structure of English" ' (Fries, 1952), *Lg.*, Vol. 31, No. 2, 1955, 335–345

Smith, F. and Miller, G. A. (1966) *The Genesis of Language*, M.I.T.

Society for Pure English (1919) *Tract No. 1*: Preliminary Announcement and List of Members, Oct., 1919

Sonnenschein, E. A. (1911) *Joint Committee on Grammatical Terminology: Report, On the Terminology of Grammar*, London

Spearman, C. (1923) *The Nature of Intelligence and the Principles of Cognition*, New York

Spencer, J. and Gregory, M. J. (1964) *An Approach to the Study of Style*, in Enkvist, Spencer and Gregory (1964), London

Spiker, C. C. (1963) *Verbal Factors in the Discrimination Learning of Children*, in Wright and Kagan (1963), 53–72

Strang, B. (1962) *Modern English Structure*, London

(1966) *Paper*, at Dartmouth (U.S.A.) Conference, quoted in Dixon (1967), 71

163

Strevens, P. D. (1965) *Papers in Language and Language Teaching*, London
(1968) *English 901*, London
(ed.) (1966) *Five Inaugural Lectures*, London
Strong, I. I. (1909) *A History of Secondary Education in Scotland*, London
Stryker, S. L. (1969) *Applied Linguistics: Principles and Techniques in Forum*, Vol. VII, No. 5, Sept–Oct 1969. (Special Issue)
Sutherland, N. S. (1966) *Discussion of Fodor and Garrett (1966)*, in Lyons and Wales (eds.) (1966) 154–163
Sweet, H. (1877) *Address to the Philological Society*, in Firth, (1964) 218
(1899) *The Practical Study of Languages*, London (reprinted, 1964)
Symonds, P. M. (1931) 'Practice Versus Grammar in the Learning of Correct English Usage', *Jour. Educ. Psy.*, Vol. XXII, Feb. 1931
Templin, M. C. (1957) *Certain Language Skills in Children: Their Development and Interrelationships*, Institute of Child Welfare Monograph Series No. 26, Minnesota
Thomas, O. (1965) *Transformational Grammar and the Teacher of English*, London
Thorne, J. (1965) 'Review of "Constituent Structure" (Postal, 1964)', *J.L.*, Vol. 1, No. 1
(1969) See Boyd and Thorne
Tibbetts, A. M. (1964) 'Two Cheers for Authoritarianism', *Coll. Eng.*, Vol. 25, No. 5, 370–373
Trager, G. L. and Smith, H. L. (1951) *An Outline of English Structure*, Battenburg
Travis, L. E. (1957) *Handbook of Speech Pathology*, New York
Trotter, A. M. (1938–40ca.) *A Manual of English Grammar*, London
Tucker, G. R. and Lambert, W. E. (1966) *White and Negro Listeners' Reactions to Various American-English Dialects*, (Mimeo)
Typographia (1962) Supplement: *Watching Words Move*, by Robert Brownjohn (*et al.*) in Vol. 6, Dec. 1962
Ullmann, S. (1962) *Semantics*, Oxford
Ure, J. N. (1965) *The Theory of Register and Register in Language Teaching*, Edinburgh University Work Paper, Department of English for Foreign Students
Vaugelas, C. F., Sieur de (1647) *Remarques Sur La Langue Française*, Paris
Vernon, M. D. (1962) *The Psychology of Perception*, London
Vygotsky, L. S. (1962) *Thought and Language*, M.I.T., tr. E. Hanfmann and G. Vakar
Warburg, J. (1962) *Notions of Correctness*, Supplement to Quirk (1962), London
Watson, J. B. (1920) 'Is Thinking merely the Action of the Language Mechanisms?', *Brit. Jour. Psychol.*, 1920, 11, 86–104
Wattie, J. M. (1903) *The Grammarian and his Material*, English Association Pamphlet, No. 75, London
Webster's Third New International Dictionary (1961), Springfield
Wells, R. (1947a) 'Immediate Constituents', *Lg.*, Vol. 23, No. 2, 1947, 81–117

(1947b) 'De Saussure's System of Linguistics', *Word*, Vol. 3, 1–2, Aug. 1947, 1–31

(1960) *Nominal and Verbal Style*, in Sebeok (1960)

Wertheimer, M. (1945) *Productive Thinking*, New York

Wheeler, D. (1958) 'Studies in the Development of Reasoning in Schoolchildren', *Brit. Jour. Statistical Psych.*, Vol. XI, Pt. II, Nov. 1958

Whitehall, H. (1968) *Structural Essentials of English*, Longman, London

Whitehead, F. (1966) *The Disappearing Dais*, London

Wilkinson, A. M. (1964) *Research on Formal Grammar*, N.A.T.E. Bulletin, I, 24–26

(*et al.*) (1965) *Spoken English*, Educ. Rev., Occasional Publications, No. 2, Birmingham

Williams, A. M. (1897) *The Scottish School of Rhetoric*, London

Williams, M. M. (1958) 'Number Readiness', *Educ. Rev.*, Birmingham, Nov. 1958

Wilsden, L. W. (1906) *The Teaching of English Grammar and Elementary Latin*, London

Wilson, G. (ed.) (1967) *A Linguistics Reader*, London

Wiseman, S. (1961) *The Efficiency of Examinations*; in Wiseman, S. (ed.) *Examinations and English Education*, Manchester

Wittrock, M. C. (1963) 'Verbal Stimuli in Concept Formation – Learning by Discovery', *Jour. Educ. Psy.*, Vol. 54, No. 4, 183–190

Wolfe, D. M. (*et al.*) (1966) *Enjoying English* (Teachers' Manual for Book 12), New York

Wright, J. C. and Kagan, J. (1963) *Basic Cognitive Processes in Children*, Monograph of the Society for Research in Child Development, Ser. No. 86, Vol. 28, No. 2, 1963

165

# Abbreviations used in Bibliography

| | |
|---|---|
| Archivum Linguisticum | Arch. L. |
| British Journal of Psychology | Brit. Jour. Psychol. |
| British Journal of Educational Psychology | Brit. Jour. Educ. Psy. |
| British Journal of Statistical Psychology | Brit. Jour. Statistical Psychol. |
| Bulletin of the National Association of Secondary School Principals | Bull. Nat. Assoc. Sec. Sch. Princ. |
| College English | Coll. Eng. |
| Educational Review | Educ. Rev. |
| Education Studies of the University of Iowa | Univ. Iowa, Stud. Educ. |
| Elementary School Journal | Elem. Sch. Jour. |
| English Language Teaching | E.L.T. |
| Harvard Educational Review | H.E.R. |
| Journal of Child Psychology and Psychiatry | Jour. Ch. Psychol. and Psychiatry |
| Journal of Educational Psychology | Jour. Educ. Psy. |
| Journal of Educational Research | Jour. Educ. Res. |
| Journal of Linguistics | J.L. |
| Journal of Social Issues | Jour. Soc. Issues |
| Language | Lg. |
| Language and Speech | Lang. and Sp. |
| Lingua | Ling. |
| Linguistic Reporter | Ling. Rep. |
| Modern Languages Association | M.L.A. |
| Modern Languages Journal | M.L.J. |
| National Association of Teachers of English | N.A.T.E. |
| Quarterly Journal of Speech | Quar. Jour. Sp. |
| Review of English Literature | Rev. Eng. Lit. |
| Scottish Council for Research in Education | S.C.R.E. |
| Scottish Education Department | S.E.D. |
| Scottish Secondary Teachers Association | S.S.T.A. |
| Times Educational Supplement (Scottish Edition) | T.E.S. (Scot.) |
| Transactions of the Philological Society | T.P.S. |

# Index

167

168

169

170

# Index of Names referred to in the text

175

**Applied Linguistics and Language Study**

**General Editor : CN Candlin**